PINK HEALS

THE MENDING OF AMERICA

Dave Graybill

with

Lance Zedric

PINK HEALS

THE MENDING OF AMERICA

ISBN 978-0-9838361-0-0

Cover photo by Paul Markow
Design by Russ Blaise
      & Ching Zedric

Printed in the United States of America

DEDICATION

To my mom—the best mother a son could ever have. Thank you for loving me unconditionally and for never limiting my dreams. Love, your son.

~

To my children—the joys of my life—you make every day an adventure and a blessing. Love, dad.

~

And to women everywhere—you are the power that heals. Love, Dave.

Acknowledgments

Thousands of people had a part in this book. They are the family, friends, coaches, mentors, teammates, and anonymous souls who have loved, shaped, taught, and touched me deeply. They have enriched my life and brought me joy at every turn, and they have my sincere and eternal gratitude. Foremost, I want to acknowledge Lisa Stevens, the backbone behind the entire *Pink Heals Program*. Lisa was with me before day one, and continues to be the most important person in the organization. She is my best friend, advisor, confidant, and sometimes boss. Without her creative talents and solid business sense, the apparel that buys the fuel that moves the trucks that inspire the volunteers who help the people, would not have been created. Without her, the program would not be where it is today. She has my back. And my heart.

Lisa and me

CONTENTS

FOREWORD

My name is Dave Graybill, and you have never met anyone like me. I am not famous, although I might be someday. I am not a superstar athlete, although I played professional baseball and was on the U.S. Olympic Baseball Team. And I am certainly not rich, because money has never mattered. I am just a retired firefighter for the city of Glendale, Arizona. Employee number 06310. I rode on a truck for 22 years and worked a common job. But I am extraordinary in one way. In 2007, I founded the *Cares Enough to Wear Pink/Pink Heals Program*, which tours the country in pink fire trucks celebrating women and helping to raise money to battle the terrorist called cancer. And I care like nobody else.

For the record, nobody in my family is suffering from or has died from cancer. My mother is still living and she is the light of my life. No special friends or beloved teachers have succumbed to the disease, nor have I lost anyone close to it. So why did I create a program to fight cancer? Why do I spend three months a year on the road touring? And why do I give away my program for free? Love. I love people. I love life. And I love making a difference. I have no hidden agenda nor ulterior motive. My gift has always been the ability to create something that is selfless, and having the drive and endurance to make it work. But my greatest gift is the ability to inspire others to do great things.

I believe that men are warriors, and that our purpose on earth is to protect our women, children, homes, and communities against anyone or anything that may harm them. I created the *Pink Heals Program* knowing that pink fire trucks symbolize hope, love, care, and rescue, and I believe that women are the most selfless creatures on the planet. If we love, honor, and provide for them, they will return that love tenfold. I believe that everything runs through a woman's heart, symbolized by the color pink, and that everything that is sick or broken can be healed through her.

The *Pink Heals Program* is far-reaching and has had an enormous impact. Whether it is empowering large cities to create their own fundraising programs, or arranging for volunteers to help one woman with cancer get a wig or to have her lawn mowed, the program is dedicated to serving the women we love. It is growing so large and so fast that it is impossible to define everything it encompasses in a few sentences or even in an entire book. But despite its growth, the program is simple and its results are clear.

In four years, the *Cares Enough to Wear Pink/Pink Heals Program* and its pink fire trucks has logged over 70,000 miles and traveled to over 200 cities spreading hope and raising awareness. In less than 16 months, more than 30 Pink Heals chapters have been formed in the United States and in Canada, with more in the process at home and abroad. We have only begun to tap our potential, but through national and regional tours and the internet, word has spread. To date, an estimated 30,000 local communities have adopted the program and have begun to wage their own battle against cancer and against all diseases that threaten the glue of our society.

So why write a book? Because the *Pink Heals Program* needs to reach more people. It needs to get greater national media exposure, to get on the Today Show and on the Ellen Show, and into the halls of Congress. It needs a calling card that introduces the program to the general public and serves as a medium that can inform and educate in the home. We need a book to grow.

It is my hope that this book will make you laugh a little, cry a lot, and inspire you to do more. It is part autobiography and part motivational how-to. The first two chapters explore my upbringing and my formative years, and focus on my career as a college and professional athlete. What does this have to do with Pink Heals? A lot. Genetics and competitive athletics are what made me the way I am, and that is central to the creation and success of the program. Early chapters also examine the beginnings of my life as a firefighter and the creation of the Golf Across The USA Tour, which launched a conflicting career in philanthropy.

The middle chapters describe the formation of the *Cares Enough to Wear Pink/Pink Heals Program*. They explain how a national movement began with a simple pink tee shirt and a two-ton stainless steel ribbon, and grew into the 2008 *Pink Ribbon Tour*, and then evolved into the yearly *Pink Heals Tour*.

The final third of the book is the most important section and explains the step-by-step process of how to start a local Pink Heals chapter or how to implement the program in your own community. Essentially, it is a how-to guide to developing a fundraising program at the grass roots level that ensures that all the money raised within a community stays in that community and helps women who are battling cancer and other diseases.

I have tried to include as many photographs as possible throughout the book to help the reader make a visual connection to the story. There have been literally thousands of photos taken of our pink fire trucks and of the courageous women battling cancer who have attended our events across the nation, and some are more powerful and inspirational than any written word. I encourage everyone to visit my Facebook page and to view the over 1000 photos that appear there, and to check out the Pink Heals website at *www.pinkfiretrucks.org* to see when the *Pink Heals Tour* will be in your area. But first, enjoy the book.

-Dave

INTRODUCTION

Two unrelated events led me to discover what I was meant to do in life. The first was 9-11, and the second was the death of my father. Each, in its own way, affected me differently, but the impact of their confluence was profound. For too long my life had been all about me. About what I had done. And about what I had wanted. I was not greedy or selfish, but like many elite athletes who are used to being idolized, pampered, and applauded, I became self-centered. And I didn't like it. I had finally arrived at a point in my life where it was time to put others first.

On the morning of September 11, 2001, I watched in horror as the Twin Towers in New York City crumbled into a fiery mass of pulverized concrete and twisted steel. Like millions of Americans, I was stunned and appalled by the loss of human life and by the utter destruction wreaked upon our country by the cowardly act of terrorists. I felt helpless and angry. But what could I do? I was a common firefighter sitting on my ass in Phoenix, Arizona, enjoying a comfortable life, while in New York City, the whole world was crashing in. I had never felt so useless as a man and as a human being. Whatever I was doing, it was not enough.

For a couple months after the bombing, I kept thinking about how public safety and other great organizations had come together to help people. I was moved by America's patriotism and proud of how my fellow firefighters, police, and President George W. Bush supported the city of New York. Such an outpouring of humanity and selflessness by others inspired me to devise a plan for firefighters to help children. I had just watched the movie *Forrest Gump*, and I was moved by the scene where Gump runs across the country after the death of his mother gaining crowds of dedicated but puzzled followers. I was struck by why the people followed him. Clearly, it was not because of money or recognition, but because they just assumed that whatever Gump was doing, he was doing it for the right reasons. They just needed to believe in something greater than themselves and to reach for some higher meaning beyond what lay within their grasp. Or maybe it was what I needed. I didn't know. But the answer would come.

CHAPTER 1
PLAY BALL

I love a challenge. When I was eight years old, I attempted to break the world record for consecutive jumps on a pogo stick without falling off. At that time, the mark stood at about 100,000 jumps, which I clearly saw as attainable, but at that age, it was unlikely I realized how many that was. One summer's day, after I had been in front of the house jumping for almost four hours and ignoring repeated calls to dinner, my mom sprang into action. She darted outside and chased me around the yard with a yardstick until I fell off, effectively ending my pogo stick career and dreams of glory. After that, I taught myself to ride a unicycle because it was more challenging and dangerous than riding a skateboard or a bicycle. I got so good at it that I would ride atop the six-foot high concrete block fences that skirted the houses in our neighborhood. The blocks were only eight inches wide, but I loved racing over them. I was never really a daredevil, but when I put my mind to something, I wanted to be the best. And I still do.

I get my competitive spirit from my dad, Dave Graybill, Sr., and like most boys growing up, I was more afraid of my father than anyone or anything in the whole world. I grew up like that and it created the perfect storm in me—that combination of competitive spirit, drive, and an absolute hatred of losing. That's what I'm all about.

The Pink Panthers. My first baseball team. Coincidence?
I don't think so. I'm in the front row far left.

My father grew up in Harrisburg, Pennsylvania and was voted among the top 100 athletes ever to come out of the state. He went to John Harris High School and was raised by an aunt. Instead of getting into trouble, he turned to athletics to get him out of a dysfunctional environment. He earned a scholarship to Arizona State University, where he became one of the greatest athletes in the school's history. He lettered 11 out of a possible 12 times in football, basketball, and baseball, which is virtually unheard of in major college athletics, and is a member of ASU's Sports Hall of Fame. He still holds the school record for pass completion percentage in football, and was an All-Border Conference first-team forward in basketball. In baseball, he pitched, played third base and outfield, and led the team in batting three successive seasons from 1955-57. He finished with a career .392 batting average, which was second all-time at ASU to that point. He was also part of ASU history. In 1955, he played in their first night game, and also hit three home runs and had six RBI against Wyoming. He was the only Sun Devil to hit three home runs in a single game during the early baseball era from 1907-1958, and not only that, he won a national championship in men's handball.

After college, my dad was drafted by the then New York Giants Baseball Team and played in the minor leagues during the 1957 season, which he thoroughly disliked. After college, the Chicago Bears courted him to play professional football, but he opted to play baseball instead of trying to make a team that was loaded with talent at his position. Given his need for routine and regimentation, he was ill suited for the long and grueling travel, uncomfortable motels, poor food, and uncertainty associated with life on the road, and he quit after one season. However, that same need suited him well in the Army National Guard, where he retired as a colonel, but it sometimes made life difficult for us kids, especially in the summers, because he always woke before 5 a.m., and always woke us to be up with him. My dad was the *Great Santini* in some ways, but I owe him a lot. He died in 2002 at the age of 67.

My parents met while they were in college. On the outside, they were the perfect couple. He was a sports star and she was a Scandinavian beauty with brains. They fell in love and started a family. My sister, Dalene, is the oldest, followed by me, then my brother, Darren. We all grew up in Tempe, and my sister and I went to Tempe High School, while my brother attended Corona Del Sol. But our lives were not idyllic.

When I was young, my parents struggled in their marriage. Mom taught school and dad was a developer. He worked constantly, always came home mad, and showed little affection. He was neither a hugger nor an acknowledger of a job well done, and nothing was ever good enough. He always critiqued and criticized what we did, no matter how important or how insignificant, and he demanded excellence in everything. And although he hated bullies, he had a tendency to be one, especially when he was drinking.

My family

I inherited my athletic ability from my father. Even as a young kid, I was good at every game and sport I tried, especially if it involved a ball, and I often played against kids several years older. All I needed was a little practice, and if I was not the best, my competitive nature took over and I worked until I was. But my father's presence was very intimidating. In stature, he was big and strong, and in the community, he was revered, so I grew up with a strong pressure to perform at a high level. "I know your father," people would say. "If you're anything like him you're going to be one helluva player."

They were right, but it was not easy being the namesake of a man whose athletic accomplishments were larger than life. When I was 11 years old and my brother was nine, my dad attended one of our little league games, but for some unknown reason my coach yanked me out of the game and replaced me with my brother. Then the coach yanked him out. My dad, who was helping coach the team, was sitting in the dugout and said something to the coach, who responded sarcastically. For whatever reason, my dad stormed out of the dugout and went home. At home later that night, my coach came over and spoke with my father, and their conversation got heated. My dad exploded and chased my coach out the front door and tackled him in our bushes. He then grabbed him by the throat and slammed him up against the garage. It was chaos and I didn't know what to do. People came from all over the neighborhood and eventually calmed my dad down. He never coached again.

I grew up in a household that was extremely judgmental. Performance, looks, character, money, education. Everything was critical. Whenever I would bring a friend home my dad would grill him about his grades and what his dad did for a living. If my dad decided that my friend was not the kind of person he wanted around me, I was forbidden to hang out with him. Dad was the same when it came to girls, always instructing me to find a girl at the athletic track and to ensure that she was tall and athletic.

My mom was the polar opposite of my dad and a savior to us all. She was always getting my siblings and me involved in something. I was task oriented and did not always like what she got me into, but once I was in, I was committed to doing my best. One time, she signed me up for a used book drive to support the local library. I collected almost 700 books, while the next closest kid collected less than 30. Another time, she enrolled me in country dancing lessons at the local athletic club so she could have a practice partner. She also taught me how to cook and to bake. When I first learned how to make angel food cake, I made it three or four times a day, and I even learned how to cook Swedish pancakes and other traditional Scandinavian dishes. Every day was limited only by my imagination, and my mother always allowed me to explore new horizons and to try different things. She taught me how to macramé and how to make jewelry, which was a wonderful counterbalance to the physical rigors of all the sports that I was playing. I would sit contentedly for hours each day making macramé pots and jewelry. I even won an arts festival award in the 7th grade for a pendant that I made for my mom, and to this day, I think she is prouder of that than of any of my athletic accomplishments.

I was lucky to have a strong support system outside

Mom and me

of my family that began with my 7th grade basketball coach, Wynn Chadwick. At that time, my parents were increasingly having marital issues, and it was affecting me. They would come home and argue constantly, and I withdrew into myself and turned into a selfish brat who didn't care about anyone else. I had a bad attitude, and my coach saw trouble coming. He was about 6'4 and a giant of a man, and I think he talked to my mom, who taught at the same school, and planned a "change of attitude" session to help turn me around. One day after basketball practice, he took me behind the bleachers and stuck his finger in my chest without raising his voice. When I talked back, he shoved me with both hands and knocked me on my ass and made me cry. "I'm not afraid of your father," he said. "I could care less who he is, but I'm not going to let you waste your potential and ruin your future. If you don't straighten up and stop being so selfish, I'm going to go to your father, and if I have to fight him, I'll do it."

That shove changed my life. From then on, I was the

consummate team player and tried to make everyone around me better. I showed up early to practice, never said anything negative, and every time on the basketball court, I passed to the open man. My coach saved me. He and my mom. Not my dad. It was not the four-sport superstar—*The Great Santini*. My mom helped me become a man. And for that, I love her.

My Own Man

In high school, I was a three-sport athlete and the typical All-American kid. I dressed well, kept my room neat and clean, and was an average B-C student. If I was passionate about a class or something that I was interested in, I excelled at it, but if it didn't interest me

Pitching for Tempe High School.

or if my heart wasn't in it, I had difficulty focusing and applying myself. I am the same way today. However, I never had trouble focusing on sports.

After a successful high school career in which I played football, basketball, and baseball, I earned a full athletic scholarship to Arizona State University to play baseball. It was the perfect fit. I got to attend one of the best baseball colleges in the nation in my own hometown and to carry on the athletic tradition that my father had established at ASU.

College

Mark McGwire, Will Clark, and Barry Bonds are among the greatest players in the history of Major League Baseball, and when they stepped into the batter's box against me in college, I didn't know if I was going to strike them out or if they were going to hit the ball out of the park. But they didn't know if I was going to plant a fastball in their ear either. I loved the challenge of facing the best competition day in and day out, and I loved representing my teammates and coaches. But big time college baseball was no merry-go-round.

Teachers and coaches had a major impact in my life, and because of this, I am passionate about kids. Coaches like Tim Kelly, who was my pitching coach at ASU, kept me from getting into trouble, and constantly steered me in the right direction. I had so much respect and admiration for Tim that I gave him part of my signing bonus when I later signed to play professionally. If it wasn't for him, I probably wouldn't have survived college. Maybe it was because I didn't understand it at the time, but when I played at ASU, head coach Jim Brock was highly revered and was one of the winningest coaches in the history of college baseball. But what I witnessed on the field and behind the scenes was, for me, a bully system. Basically, it

On the mound for the ASU Sun Devils.

was taking young men and wringing their passion for a sport out of them like water from a dishrag. I was as competitive as anyone, but Brock's philosophy at ASU was about winning at all costs, and it rubbed me the wrong way. Although he was highly successful and was able to motivate players to perform beyond their natural abilities and expectations, winning became more important than the mission of creating good human beings. In college, I believed the mission should be about building each individual into a better man or woman, and I still believe it. On the other hand, to be a great athlete at that level and beyond, a person has to be extremely self-confident, and even narcissistic. Barry Bonds, who later became the single season and all-time home run leader in the history of Major League Baseball, was a great example. I don't necessarily think he disliked other people or spent a lot of time disliking what other people were doing, he was just so totally self-centered that all he cared about was his own performance, and it showed in everything he did. At that level, everyone is an independent contractor playing a team sport because they are judged specifically on their stats. A great player could be on a losing team and hit .500 with 50 home runs and he is going to sign a bigger professional contract than an average player on a great team.

Barry Bonds and I were teammates at ASU for two years and he was the worst teammate I ever had. He was not being paid and he was not on the team to be a good guy. And even when he was with the Pittsburgh Pirates and the San Francisco Giants, he was self-centered. His dad brought him up not to trust anybody, and later as a professional, he was paid specifically to do what he did, and he did not do one thing more. But he deserves some credit, for as much success as he had, he never partied, never drank, and never appeared in the tabloids; that is, while he was playing. He kept a close network of family and friends and rarely changed them. Now that his baseball career is over and he is mired in serious legal trouble over lying about his alleged steroid use, he probably doesn't have many close friends who've stuck by him, but he's so closed and so self-serving that he probably doesn't care. A lot of people care if people like them, but Barry is probably happy just living a private life far removed from most human contact.

Life Lesson

Baseball was everything to me at ASU, but an event that occurred outside of the sport reminded me that there was more to life than playing a game. It was a sad lesson that showed me the power of my mouth, and the impact that my words could have.

Brad Clayton was a Mormon and one of my best friends. He rented a room in a house from Len, Steve, Kenny, and Warren Shumway, who were all brothers and recently returned missionaries. Brad was moving out and knew I needed a place to stay, so he recommended that I rent from the Shumway's since they were all great guys. He also knew I needed transportation to get back and forth to school and that students were not allowed to park cars without a permit, so he sold me his Suzuki GS1000 for $1000. I rented the room and had a blast riding my motorcycle back and forth to school and to baseball practice. When I'd come home to the house, I'd rave about motorcycles and how we should all get one and start our own motorcycle club.

Steve Shumway was my roommate and the greatest person in the world. He was four or five years older than me, but we were like two peas in a pod. He was very bright and could have been anything he wanted, but he was fascinated by law enforcement and became a criminal justice major. He landscaped to pay his way through college, and when we would hang around together, he would brag about me playing baseball and I would brag about how smart he was. We had our own mutual admiration society. He was a stand-up guy and he knew that I looked up to him, so he finally bought a Yamaha sport bike so we could ride together. For several months, we zipped around and chased each other on the freeway, and had the time of our lives. But that soon changed.

Around Christmas 1982, Steve had to ride along with a police officer on the late shift in Mesa, as a requirement for a class, and because it was only 40 degrees that night, he spent an hour deciding if he should drive his truck or ride his motorcycle. Unfortunately, he made the wrong choice. As he was heading home around 3 a.m., he stopped at a traffic light, and a man who was driving around in a pickup truck looking for his girlfriend who he thought was cheating on him, ran a red light and ran him over, killing him instantly.

The family was devastated, and so was I. The family was so distraught that they left Steve's wrecked motorcycle in the garage and his belongings sitting in a bag in the kitchen for days. It was heartbreaking. From the tragic loss of my friend, I learned that we can never fully know the impact of what we say or how we say it, and that it is important to measure our words. Hence, I never got on a motorcycle again and always watched my mouth.

After Steve's death, I realized that I was not attending college for an education. It was all about baseball at ASU. In fact, upon arriving on campus, someone selected most of my classes for me, and if not, certain classes came "highly recommended." Also, as a scholarship athlete, I didn't have many other school responsibilities, because high profile athletes are large investments that can be pay great dividends, and we couldn't be overworked unless it was on the field. Although I was sometimes dissatisfied with certain aspects of college, ASU was still my single best route to a professional baseball career.

Despite the win-at-all-cost atmosphere, I thrived at ASU. My junior year I went 10-0 with 11 saves, just one off the all-time record, and earned Honorable Mention All Pac-10. Our team entered the College World Series ranked #1 with a 53-18 record and had high hopes of winning a national title. We beat Miami 9-6 in our opening game, and I earned a save. We then routed #2 ranked Oklahoma State 23-12 in a record-setting win, but we were beaten by Texas and then eliminated by Cal State Fullerton, the eventual national champion. The final month of the 1984 season was incredible. Despite our loss in the College World Series, we had finished the regular season ranked #1, and I had been selected in the Major League Baseball Draft and was preparing for the chance of competing in the 1984 Olympic Games in Los Angeles. It was truly the best of times.

National Team

Getting selected to participate on the 1984 U.S. National Men's Baseball team, which would become the 1984 Olympic team, was a great honor. Initially, I didn't know I was going to be selected because the selection committee was only going to pick 24 guys, and from what I understood, I wasn't going to be one of them. So, I called Rod Dedeaux, the head coach of the Olympic team and the coach at rival USC, from a pay phone and left a long message, "This is Dave Graybill. I am the short reliever on ASU. I don't know if you've picked the team yet, but there's no reason why I shouldn't be on it. These are my stats. I'll send you a video."

It wasn't long before I got a call back. Since the regular season was still going on, the coach said that he would come to Tempe and watch me pitch against the University of North Carolina, ranked #3 in the nation at the time, while we were ranked #1. We had Barry Bonds and Oddibe McDowell, and they had Scott Bankhead and B.J. Surhoff, and I threw five innings of shutout ball and struck out nine batters. I owned them, and so the next day he called and said, "You're on the Olympic team." We were the first U.S. Olympic Baseball Team to be formed since 1964, and ironically, Dedeaux, also was the head coach of that team.

Getting selected to the Olympic Team wasn't a big deal to me at the time because the way I was raised by my father, making it was something I was supposed to do. Perhaps that dulled the luster somewhat, but actually touring the country with the Olympic Baseball Team was a heady experience. Although I had twice played in the College World Series and was a member of one of the premier collegiate baseball programs in the nation, there was something special about the notion of playing for my country. One of my fondest memories was when the team was given a private tour of the Baseball Hall of Fame in Cooperstown, New York, and we were asked to signed several items for the museum. None of us knew what the hell we were signing, because most of the time we just did what we were told. Every so often, something with our signatures appears for sale on Ebay, which is kind of surreal. The next day, we played an exhibition game at Abner Doubleday Stadium. Several years later, I took my son to Cooperstown, and we visited a memorabilia store, and told the guy working there the story about the 1984 Olympic Team visiting. "I remember you guys," he exclaimed. "You were sitting with McGwire and Will Clark, and we bought your lunch at the restaurant across the street." Small world.

Unfortunately, my Olympic experience ended abruptly a short time before the opening ceremonies, when I was removed from the roster because of an injury. A week before the Games I injured my thigh so badly that I was unable to put any weight on my leg, much less to pitch, so the decision made sense. But it was still one of the greatest disappointments of my life. My embarrassment was compounded because stories about me making the team had already appeared in several newspapers, including my hometown paper, *The Arizona Republic*. Even worse, I felt that I let myself and my friends and family down. That was the most difficult part of the process. But I still feel a strong kinship with the guys on the Olympic team. We had some wonderful players, including future stars Mark McGwire, Will Clark, Barry Larkin, B.J. Surhoff, Bobby Witt, Norm Charlton, Billy Swift, and others. All of the players were drafted by professional baseball teams and enjoyed wonderful careers. With that much talent, and with the Games being in Los Angeles, there was a lot of pressure on us to win, but we were upset by Japan 6-3 in the championship game. Although I never got to participate in the actual Games with Team USA, I still consider myself an Olympian.

Pro Baseball

A baseball player is never happy until he has made the big leagues. Whether they're playing in Triple-A or at a prodigious collegiate powerhouse like ASU, or even in the College World Series, a player wants to be in the big leagues more than anything else, and I was no different. But I fell just short. I'm not a religious person, but God gave me an ability and put me here to do exactly what I'm doing right now. Baseball was just a tool to gain experience and to build confidence and self-esteem. I would never trade my love for people for a professional baseball career. Gratifying myself by striking out people is pretty small in the larger context of life, but as a young, soon-to-be professional baseball player with the world at my feet, I didn't exactly see it that way at the time.

I was drafted by the Montreal Expos as the 41st pick in the 1984 Major League Baseball June Amateur Draft, and was sandwiched between the Texas Rangers' Jimmy Meadows and Scott Wade of the Boston Red Sox. I signed for $60,000, which was decent money at the time, but nothing compared to the millions that many of today's players receive directly out of high school. Naturally, my personal expectations and the professional expectations of the Expos were high. At the professional level, everything is about individual statistics and winning today.

After the Olympics in Los Angeles, I reported to the Single-A West Palm Beach Expos of the Florida League, where I went 2-2 with a 2.39 ERA. The following spring,

My own baseball cards!

I spent a few weeks in the Instructional League in St. Petersburg, Florida before reporting to spring training. After spring training I was promoted to AA ball with the Jacksonville Expos of the Southern League and became a teammate of pitcher Randy Johnson, who is a lock for the Major League Baseball Hall of Fame when he becomes eligible in 2014. Randy was drafted in the second round of the 1985 draft out of the University of Southern California, and was blessed with immense physical talent. We would go to spring training every year with some of the best players in baseball, and although most of us got along well, the competition was cutthroat. Every player had been a high school or college superstar and a great all-around athlete in several sports. Contrary to what a lot of people say, baseball players are great athletes too. Like my father, I was well rounded. I could throw a football 70 yards and had good speed and quickness, and loved to play basketball. During spring training, the players would challenge each other at golf, pool, darts, cards, and about any other game. To the average person that might not be a big deal, but when you have people whose entire lives are about competing and owning up to their abilities, even playing pop-a-shot and arcade games over a few beers was competitive. Gary Wayne, who pitched for the Colorado Rockies and the Minnesota Twins, loved to play Elevator Action. We played it every night, and it helped keep us out of trouble.

But pickup basketball was probably the most competitive game we played at spring training. We'd play on the outdoor park courts in West Palm Beach where a breeze blew 24 hours a day. It was so windy that a jump shooter would have to shoot the ball two or three feet to the left just to sink it. Most of us could eventually gauge our shots based on the breeze, but a power forward or an inside guy definitely had the advantage. And that was Randy.

Randy was an outstanding athlete and a great person, but was often misread as a person. He was an introvert and carried himself a certain way, and he didn't like to be bothered. But if he liked a person, he'd develop a connection and show an unbelievable heart. But when in competitive mode, he was a warrior. And it was that warrior mentality and menacing demeanor that contributed to 22 years in Major League Baseball and a career that ranks among the best in the history of the game. But back in the day, he always wore headphones and listened to acid rock in his own world, so I'd lure him into an argument about our colleges or about basketball. He's 6'10 and I'm 6'2, and he'd always brag about how USC recruited him to play basketball, so one day I challenged him to play one-on-one in West Palm Beach, where the breeze was blowing about 30 miles per hour. As usual, I was trying to gauge my shots in the wind, while like a typical big man, he backed me down to within three feet of the basket. I hate to admit it, but he beat me 10-9. I didn't lose often, but he was the better man that day. I bet he still thinks about that to this day, because there is something great and very basic about two guys going one-on-one on a court in the middle of nowhere. In a funny way, it is reminiscent of the classic television commercial in the 1980s where Magic Johnson of the Los Angeles Lakers arrives by limousine in rural French Lick, Indiana to play one-on-one against Larry Bird of the Boston Celtics. Randy, I want a rematch!

The 1985 season was also an eye-opener. Tommy Thompson was the first manager I had that was an in-your-face type of guy. He was a stiff-legged, heavy smoking, middle-aged, out-of-control, Nazi-type manager who used to scream, "I'm going to allow Graybill to punch my ass because he's nothing but a f_ _ _king pussy! C'mon pussy, punch me!"

He always wanted to provoke a fight. Whether it was a test or he was serious, nobody knew. He would call a player out in the locker room in front of everybody and challenge his manhood. He would light a cigarette and blow smoke in your face just to get a reaction or get into your face like a drill sergeant. Given my dislike for bullies, he and I didn't mesh well, and it was the first time in my life that I saw this side of baseball. Playing baseball at ASU was like riding in a gilded limo compared to the minor leagues. Not only were the coaches a different level, but the players as well. Some of the players in the minor leagues were fresh off the tractor and looked at players from elite programs with awe. There were several guys fresh out of high school, Latino players who could barely speak English, collegiate players, and older players who were on their way back down. But the experience was more positive than negative.

In May, I was called up from Double-A to pitch in the Pearson Cup at the Olympic Stadium in Montreal, which featured the two Canadian Major League Baseball teams, the Montreal Expos and the Toronto Blue Jays. The annual mid-season exhibition game was played from 1978-1986, and helped raise money for minor league baseball in Canada. The game was halted in 1986, but was brought back in 2003, and is now part of interleague play.

The game I pitched in went into extra innings, but because both teams had to get back on the road to resume their regular schedule, it ended in a rare tie 2-2. I pitched two scoreless innings and even got a base hit, but I felt a pop in my shoulder while pitching. Because I didn't come out of the game, the clicking got progressively worse. It didn't hurt, but I knew something was wrong. The next day my shoulder was sore. Although I didn't know it, pitching in that game was the beginning of the end of my professional baseball career.

I began the 1986 season at Single-A ball at West Palm Beach and was promoted to the Triple-A Indianapolis Indians for their American Association Championship run. I was one step away from making the big leagues and realizing a lifelong dream. But not all dreams come true.

The following year, I started in Jacksonville, Florida in Double-A, but I felt a twinge in my elbow and finished the season on the disabled list. Dr. James Andrews, the renowned sports surgeon, diagnosed my injury and recommended that I have Tommy John surgery to repair damaged ligaments in my elbow, but I decided against surgery and was shut down for the rest of that season and for entire 1988 season. It was the first time I had not played organized baseball since I was a kid, so I decided to retire. The coach and some of the brass thought that my pitching career was over and that I would be better served as a pitching coach, but I just wanted to go home and clear my head. It was hard to take knowing that the Expos were no longer interested in me as a player.

Back in Arizona, I took a job in real estate with the Leo Eisenberg Company, and began working out again. My arm started to feel better and I began to have second thoughts about retirement. In the meantime, I got Chris Beasley, a former ASU teammate, a tryout with Joe Madden, one of the California Angels minor league instructors at the time. Joe, who is the current manager of the Tampa Bay Devil Rays, signed Chris on the spot, and Chris made it to the big leagues in 1991. The whole process looked too easy. I knew I could still pitch, but I needed to convince the Expos to give me my release, which they did. Knowing they didn't want me as a pitcher led to my decision to tryout for the Angels.

In 1989, I signed with Palm Springs, the Angels Single-A affiliate. I went 7-2 and was promoted to Double-A in Midland, Texas, where I compiled a 4-4 record. I pitched 130 innings that year, the most in my professional career, but it took a toll on my body. Early in the season, I was a starter and my arm felt great, but when they moved me to Midland and made me a reliever, my elbow started hurting. I was tired of the training room and started taking heavy doses of anti-inflammatory medicine. I felt that I was too old to have surgery and I had tremendous guilt about playing baseball while my wife was home with our young daughter, Lauren. At 27 years of age, I was beginning to see the writing on the wall. That is the prime age for most baseball players, and if they haven't made it to the big leagues by then, the odds are against ever making it. Only 1 out of 100,000 people who play baseball ever play one game in the major leagues. I had become a statistic.

A New Career

I never imagined that I would be a firefighter. I always knew that I would become a famous Major League Baseball player and live the American dream. I would be wildly successful, financially well off, and totally fulfilled. I would be loved and admired by everyone and each day would be better than the next. But life has a way of punching you in the jaw and dropping you to your knees. I forgot to duck.

In early 1985, I got married. And like most couples starting out, we had our ups and downs and tried hard to carve out a life, but my chasing a dream was hard on our marriage. I was gone half of each year playing baseball and money was tight. After the 1989 season, my injuries become more prevalent, and I realized that I had better start thinking about life after baseball. But what could I do? I had dropped out of college and I did not have a degree, and the nomadic lifestyle of a minor league baseball player became increasingly tough. I needed a career that offered more stability and the opportunity to spend more time at home with my family. Firefighting also provided a high-adrenaline atmosphere and the sense of teamwork and camaraderie that I had enjoyed in sports. But at its core, it was rooted in public service, and that's what attracted me most.

When I finally decided that I wanted to be a firefighter, I attacked getting hired like I was pitching against Mark McGwire. Hard and fast. Like many A-type personalities, I have a little Attention Deficit Hyperactivity Disorder (ADHD) when it comes to waiting for something I want, so I immediately took the initiative and discovered which fire departments were testing. A Mesa firefighter said to let him know who I was testing with, so I did, and he called someone in the Glendale Fire Department and recommended me. Over 2700 applicants tested for only three spots, so I took the test and got hired. One minute I'm a former professional baseball player turned real estate agent, then three months later, I'm hired as a firefighter. I entered Fire Academy Class 90-1 on February 12, 1990, and sixteen weeks later, I graduated. The classes were longer at that time because we earned our EMT certification while at the academy. Over the next four

Fire Academy graduation photo.

years, I continued to learn my trade but kept baseball in the back of my mind. In 1993 my son, Dave, was born. I had it all; a respectable job, two great children, and a beautiful and loving wife.

My wife loved being married to a firefighter and we

were a family on the go. I had just given up a selfish dream and was creating a normal life for my family. I was saving for retirement and providing security. On the outside, we were the perfect couple, but as many couples, we grew apart as man and wife, then as friends. My wife was a calm, centered naturalist, and I was an adventurous, hyperactive person who wanted to push the envelope in everything I did, and it was that nature that made me feel trapped in my own house. After a while, I was just going through the motions. I would mow the lawn, pick the kids up, and go to work. Then I would come home and she would go to work. We could never just relax, have fun, and enjoy each other.

I grew up in a home that was very tense and it was seldom a place of safety and comfort. I enjoyed being out of the house, especially when my dad was home, because he often bullied everyone and that created a constant state of conflict within the family. When I got married, I wanted my own home to be a place of refuge and love. I thrived on the constant hugging and kissing and affection in our young family, but when the routine of life crept in and the passion went out of my marriage, I felt the tension in my own home grow. I feared that it would become like my boyhood home, and I didn't want that for my children.

One afternoon at home, I happened to watch the Oprah Show, and the topic was couples staying together. The guest psychologist told the audience to look at their mate of 25 years and to ask themselves if they could or wanted to travel across the country in a mobile home with that person. It was a defining moment in my life. I looked across the table at my wife, who I had not been getting along with for some time, and decided that I wanted out of the marriage. It wasn't fair to her, me, or to the kids. I had grown up in a home where the love had died, and I believed it would be better for everyone if I left. I loved having kids with her, and she was a great mother and a good person, but I could not see myself being with her for the rest of my life.

My marriage ended in 1994, and it was one of the most difficult times in my life. My ex is a wonderful person and a great mother, but as with many married couples, we were unable to work through our problems. When I got divorced, I lost everything, but I pushed for our kids to get a white-collar education while maintaining blue-collar values. Being a divorced firefighter and having kids is tough because the system makes it difficult. It is hard to be the father you want to be and to spend time with your kids when you have to work a second or third job just to pay bills. At the time of my divorce, I was working 56 hours a week and making $27,500 a year. With child support taken out of my paychecks, I netted about $150 every two weeks, barely enough to live on. Firefighters work a 24-hour shift on, and then have 48 hours off. In the two days between shifts, I could have worked a second job or started another career, but I would have been without my children for three days a week, six if station time was included, and that was unacceptable. Also, I could have worked my other two days off to pay bills and to have my own home, but that would also deny me time with my kids. I decided not to do that. Instead, I lived on nothing. When the kids were in school, I got my real estate license and tried to open a restaurant, but my heart wasn't in it.

For the next few years after my divorce, I was basically living and raising my kids in my grandma's 1989 Cavalier station wagon, which we later nicknamed "The Dugout," because the over-30 baseball league I was playing in used it as a mobile dugout to carry our balls, bats, food, and everything else. It was an ugly tan color and was essentially my zip code for six months. My grandma had died, so my mom gave it to me so I could commute to work. I would pick my kids up from their mother's house, take them to my favorite coffee shop, and hang out. I would introduce them to my friends and take them to the Village Athletic Club, where we would play basketball, racquetball, and other games for several hours. It was great fun and my kids

My kids and me in Chicago. Priceless!

and I loved it. How many families get to play together like that and in what better environment? It was like a second home for my children and me. There were so many good people in my life that helped me raise my children. I would like to take all the credit, but I can't. From my ex-wife to Lisa Stevens, to Frank Johnson to

B.B. Fontonet, and to Matt Ingram to Steve Jackson and all the other great coaches and people who have played such an important role in my children's lives, thank you.

During one especially difficult time, my friend Paul Markow, approached me and asked if I wanted to try commercial modeling. I was in my early 30s and wasn't a model type guy, but he believed that I could make money doing it, so he told me what to do and how to do it. I took his advice and went out and spent what little money I had on clothes and had photos taken. Soon, I got a call from a talent agency that wanted me to audition for a Southwest Airlines commercial in which they needed a pitcher to throw a home run pitch to Chicago Cubs Hall of Famer Ryne Sandburg. He hit a home run, and then I threw my mitt on the ground and acted mad. It was the perfect gig for me because I had actual experience at giving up home runs and at getting mad after giving them up. I got the job and made $20,000, and bought my first car. In fact, I made good money from modeling for the next several years. It was great fun and I met a lot of wonderful people who would play significant roles in my life.

Replacement Player

One day in early August 1994, I was sitting at the fire station feeling about as low as I ever had, when the Major League Baseball Players Union went on strike. For me, it was a blessing in disguise. Many people in the baseball community knew I could still throw a fastball in the 90s, and that I was also a firefighter. Roger Jongewaard, the vice president of scouting and player development for the Seattle Mariners, who the year previous had asked me if I could get his son on the fire department, told me that if I ever wanted to get back into baseball, to call him. Early the next spring, the strike had not yet been resolved, so I called Roger before spring training asking for a shot with the Mariners as a Replacement Player, which was actually convenient, since the Mariners held spring training in the Phoenix area and the ball field was only a couple

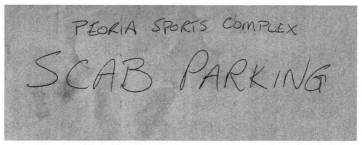

My parking permit courtesy of a fellow firefighter.

blocks away from the fire station. I was moonlighting as a professional baseball player making $1800 a month and then going into the fire station as soon as practice was over. It was the best of both worlds. But it had a downside.

Being called a "scab" isn't the glamorous side of professional sports, but amazingly, it wasn't the Major League Baseball players who protested my being a Replacement Player during the strike. It was members of my own firefighters union. And since I was a union firefighter crossing the line of a union strike, there was a lot of animosity. For Major League Baseball players to think that they're a true union when every one of them is an individual contractor is a joke, but several of the guys at the fire station were jealous of me for taking advantage of the situation, and they were pushing the union angle on me. During the strike, I would come to work at the fire station and discover "Scabs Only" signs in my parking space. But since we never played a game other than an exhibition game, which spring training games were, no one ever truly crossed the line. We would have been crossing the picket line had we flown to another city and played a game as professionals. Fortunately, the strike ended and the game I love was preserved.

Dillon and Daniele

Early one morning during spring training of the 1995 Major League Baseball strike, our fire crew got a wake up call to respond to a house fire in Peoria, Arizona. We arrived at the scene and ran into the house and discovered Dillon and Daniele Baker, twin 18-month old babies, burning alive. They were screaming in agony and we grabbed them out of their cribs. My partner took Dillon and I took Daniele. They had gruesome third degree burns on their hands and extremities, and some of their tiny fingers had been burned off, and their skin was seared and split. It was horrible. Fortunately, we were able to save them, but they would face a long, painful recovery. Afterwards, we had a debriefing at the station, but I had to leave because I was pitching at Hohokum Field against the Cubs that day. I threw two scoreless innings and we won 6-5. Larry Ward, who was a local reporter, was covering the strike and asked about my day. "I had the best and worst day of my life," I said. "What do you mean?" he asked. "I saw two burned babies, then six hours later I'm throwing against the Cubs."

Then I went through my story. "God gave me the ability to pitch. Been divorced. Got nothing. Live in my car. Saved two kids. Now I get to pitch against the Cubs. Life is life."

The story made national headlines, but more importantly, Dillon and Daniele survived. That put the importance of my job as a firefighter into perspective. Baseball is a wonderful game, but helping save lives is real, lasting, and serious, and affects so many people, that there is no comparison. I saw Dillon and Daniele for a few years after the fire, but now that they are adults, I don't see them as often as I would like. However, they often return to the burn camp that the firefighters hold. It was a life-changing experience.

One Last Chance

I pitched so well during the strike that Roger Jongewaard talked the Mariners into signing me to a contract. After the strike was over and all the other players had left, the major league manager, Lou Piniella, called me into his office and said, "I'll be goddamned if I'm not going to offer you a contract after the way you pitched. How would you like to go to Triple-A Tacoma?"

I was surprised and excited. He then says, "Can you get off work?" And I said, "Probably."

"Then get your ass to Tacoma!"

Prior to the strike, the last time I had pitched professionally was in 1989 in Double-A ball, but Piniella saw enough in me to offer me to a contract. So, I met with my fire chief and he said that as long as I could get people to cover my shifts, I could go off and play professional baseball. Two days later, I was on a plane to Tacoma. But half of the $7000 a month I earned there was spent covering my shifts at the fire department. I opened an account and had firefighters draw money out of it. In the fire service, if I had a firefighter working my shift, the city couldn't fire me.

I pitched in six games at Tacoma, but at 32 years old, I knew that this was my baseball swan song. I didn't have to leave, but I wasn't stupid. My job with the fire department was real security for my children and me, not a long-shot baseball career in which I was trying to recreate myself and take one last shot at glory. I loved playing in Tacoma, and I was on top of the world. Management even put up a booth outside Rainier Stadium that read, "The Firefighter," playing on my real job, and on the term used for baseball relief pitchers. I would sit out there and sign autographs because I was the real firefighter who had saved two kids, then later that day pitched in a professional game. It was all blown up for Major League Baseball because they were trying to promote the strike players. Life is funny. One day I was living in my grandma's station wagon, and a week later, I'm a professional baseball star sitting in my own booth at Rainier Stadium signing autographs. It was a short break from the tough situation I had put myself in, and I made the best of it. It was awesome.

But all good things end. Some people within the fire department and city management wanted me to stop playing baseball and to return to work. Or else. Also, my arm was beginning to hurt. If I had been throwing 95 mph with no pain and rocking Triple-A, I might have stayed, plus, a screenwriter had optioned the rights to my life story in hopes of it becoming a movie, and

I was hoping that I would earn a nice payday from it. It would have been *Back Draft* and *Bull Durham* rolled into one story; an aging ex-professional pitcher turned firefighter who makes it back to the Major Leagues after saving the lives of two children. Pure Hollywood—but true!

Very few athletes get a second chance at playing professional sports, especially when they are in their thirties and had been out of the game for as long as I had, but achieving my dream of making it to the big leagues and pitching just one inning of a regular season game, was not meant to be. It was a terrific experience and I will always be thankful to Lou Piniella and Roger Jongewaard for giving me one last shot at fulfilling my boyhood dream. But it was time to move on.

(Left) A great photo that appeared in The Arizona Republic.
(Right) My last baseball hoorah.

CHAPTER 2
MANNING UP & TEEING OFF

After retiring from professional baseball in 1995, I spent the next seven years falling short of my potential. Sure, I had a good job as a firefighter on the Glendale Fire Department, had started a construction business two years earlier, tried to open a restaurant, and worked as a part-time model, but everything I did was mostly for the wrong reasons. I was going against the natural grain of life—that unseen force or energy that ultimately compels us to do what we are meant to do, and I paid for it.

When I started Graybill Custom Homes in 1993, my goal was to become a millionaire just so I could give it all away. I'm pretty much that way with all material things, but that philosophy is rarely conducive to success in the business world. Although my construction business was relatively successful, I wasn't realizing the financial goals I had set. I learned that I had to have a partner who could do taxes and paperwork and who was detail-oriented, because it wasn't my strong suit nor did it interest me. Consequently, after two years and a few homes built, I escaped from the construction field more aware of what it took to survive and thrive in business.

Next came my brief foray into the restaurant

business, and like anything I tried, I plunged in headfirst. I created an LLC, designed a concept, mapped out a marketing strategy, raised money, hired an architect, and even found a location for the building, but when the project fell through, I realized that I needed to switch gears. My thought process needed to change from wanting to be a millionaire, to being a poor man using the energy and abilities I had, and to doing great things without money by giving of myself with the aim of creating synergy and love with other people. At the time, I didn't know what that meant, but I was compelled to do it anyway!

Golf Across The USA

The greatest epiphany of my life occurred when my dad passed away on December 24, 2002 and left me $200,000. To some that isn't much money, but to a person who didn't have any, it was a lot. I didn't want his money nor did I feel it really belonged to me, but I took it anyway, not for myself, but for others. Instead of just giving it away or blowing it on myself, I wanted to create something to bring people together to help others. I wanted to inspire people to drop whatever they were doing and to follow my cause. So, instead of running across America like Forrest Gump, I conceived the *Golf Across The USA Tour*. I wasn't a golf fanatic or even a lukewarm enthusiast. Frankly, the game was too slow for my liking, but the concept was perfect. I would personally hit a golf ball across the country and raise money for sick children. To my knowledge, no one had ever done it before, which made it even more challenging. In fact, I contacted the Guinness Book of World Records about setting the record for the longest continuous golf outing, but I squelched the idea when they said that I had to pay for around-the-clock coverage for their representatives, which included meals, hotels, travel, and everything else. I didn't need them to validate what I was about to do. I simply imagined the United States as one gigantic, 18-hole golf course with plenty of green grass, rolling hills, mountains, water, and sand traps. Literally, *Golf Across The USA* was as simple as hitting a golf ball from point A to point B. At least that's what I hoped.

In early February 2003, I sat in my favorite coffee shop trying to drum up more support for the tour. Among the patrons were several professionals and successful business people who wanted to help for no reason other than seeing my energy and believing in what I was doing, and others because they wanted to be part of something unique. And as I began explaining that the next morning I would be hitting a golf ball off the wing of a Southwest Airlines jet at the airport, a man sitting next to me, who was a western area Secret Service agent for President Bush, interrupts, "Excuse me, what exactly are you doing?"

"Southwest Airlines is going to back a big jet onto the tarmac," I explained, "and they're going to let me hit golf balls off the wing."

He looked at me like I was crazy. Because security was still high due to 9-11, he knew that the airport was not being used for anything other than legitimate reasons, and he let me know it. But I fired back. "If you don't believe me, show up at 8 o'clock and you can hit a ball off the wing too."

The agent still didn't believe me, but when I arrived at the airport the next morning, he was there waiting.

But he still couldn't believe it, so I included him in the video that was made of the event. He is the guy running down the tarmac chasing after my ball.

Teeing off on a wing and a prayer.

Teeing Up

"You can't do that! You're crazy! You'll be arrested! How are you going to do that? How are you going to shut down traffic? How are you going to get sponsors? How are you going to get permits? How are you going to convince the firefighters, police officers, mayors, city managers, and every hurried, impatient, stressed out, angry motorist from sea to shining sea to allow you do it?"

These were just a few of the hundreds of questions that friends and critics alike bombarded me with when they learned about what I was going to do. But the most common question was, "Why?" When I explained that

I was doing it for sick kids and for those suffering with Alzheimer's disease, people backed off and showed less resistance, but I still detected a strong sense of doubt.

To most people, my plan to golf across the country was either grandiose, ridiculous, or both. But to me it made perfect sense. To make the whole country my personal golf course; to hit a golf ball down Main Street USA; and to take seven months away from my job as a firefighter wasn't crazy. Well, maybe a little. But it was so crazy that when I approached corporate sponsors and charities they wanted to be part of it. *EZ-Go Golf Carts* was the first major sponsor to step up. They donated nine golf carts, while *Krispy Kreme Doughnuts* provided dozens of free donuts at each stop of the 18-city tour. *PF Changs China Bistro* was also a major contributor and donated all proceeds, totaling $150,000, from their Lettuce Wrap Day to charity. But despite the generosity of a few significant material sponsors, cash donations were minimal. Because I couldn't get anyone to donate actual money, I spent most of my inheritance funding the tour. But it was money well spent.

Right Hand Man

As the saying goes, everyone needs a good friend with which to share their misery, and Steve Kolesar was mine. Without him, *Golf Across The USA* would have never gotten off the first tee. For several months before and during the tour, he wore many hats. At different times, he was my planner, press agent, liaison, and everything between. He was the glue that held the tour together and the voice of reason when

I had lost mine. His meticulous planning, attention to detail, keen intellect, and unbridled imagination were invaluable, and I will always be grateful for his enthusiastic support and unbending belief in me and in what I was trying to accomplish. In fact, he was the only person who daily said that I could do anything I wanted and to just make it happen. I liked his way of thinking.

"Dave is truly an unusual guy who is larger than life. I've known him since he was 18. He's a very charismatic, energetic person who wants to do everything for everybody regardless of how it affects him personally. He is out there to make other peoples' lives better. He sees something that needs to be done and he goes and does it. He was constantly running ideas by me, but one day he calls and says, "Steve, I have an incredible idea, but I don't want anybody to know about it, so I really don't want to talk about it over the phone." So I invited him over, and a little later, he came in, closed the door, and sat down. "I don't want any corporate people to steal this idea from me," he began. And I said, "What is the idea?" Dave sat up. "I'm going to hit a golf ball across the United States for children's charities." I said, "What do you mean by hit a golf ball across the United States?" He said, "Nobody has ever done that before I said, "Dave, that's a helluva long way." He said, "Are you in?"

A short time later Dave copyrighted Golf Across The USA, and we began to plot the tour out. I asked him a million questions and I got a lot of blank stares and some good answers from time to time. We plotted out how he would do it, that it would be set up as an 18-hole golf course where he would tee off, golf to a location, and putt into a hole. I was probably on the phone for a year for 8-12 hours a day planning, coordinating and convincing officials from all across the country to let us come through their communities and to try to determine a trademark spot in each city that he wanted to be the putt-in and tee off.

I bought into Dave and the tour because I'm a generous guy. I like to see good people do great things that they believe in. I like to participate in unusual things that have a reason for being done, and this definitely did. I spent so much time on the tour that people were telling me that I was nuts and that I was going to lose my job. "Why are you doing this? Just stop." I said that if I stop, it stops." –Steve Kolesar

Steve Kolesar and family.

A Plan Well Made

After we had devised the basic plan for the *Golf Across The USA Tour*, Steve and I approached a large public relations firm to help with logistics, but they said that shutting down traffic in 18 major cities was impossible, and that it would cost $250,000 up front just for them to attempt to get all the permits we needed. I said, "Bullshit. I'll just do it myself." And they said, "Nobody can do that." And I said, "I'm a firefighter, watch me!"

I love to be told I can't do something. So, Steve and I dressed in our Armani suits and drove to the firefighters union convention in Las Vegas. We looked like two hit men sitting in the back of the room. After the union president spoke, we sneaked into the rear of the convention hall and intercepted him in the hallway. We stepped right in front of him and told him who we were and what we were doing, and got his signature on a letter endorsing the *Golf Across The USA Tour*, which we sent to every fire department in the country, so that the unions would help us stop traffic and provide logistical support. We did the same thing with the Fraternal Order of Police. Their union president also gave us a letter of support that was used to explain what we were doing and what we needed.

Once we received the blessing of the national union president, it was time to get the okay from our local union president and my fire chief. The biggest hurdle was covering my shifts at work for such a long period of time, a situation that I had been through in 1995 while attempting a comeback in professional baseball. However, the union and my fire chief quickly endorsed the plan when I got 67 firefighters to commit one shift for free to cover my absence. Once I received permission, Steve and I went to the city manager and mayor and presented the plan, and the city loved it because of the potential public relations value. We didn't need the city's approval since the union and fire chiefs had already given it, but it was important because we didn't want the fire chief or the union chief stepping in and taking credit for our idea.

The Front Nine

Since the entire United States was going to be my golf course, I had a lot of holes to choose from, and paring it down to 18 cities, each representing one hole, was not easy. Like all great golf courses, I wanted the United States to feature a front nine and a back nine. An average golf course ranges from 4000-6000 yards in total length and can be played in about 3-4 hours with or without a cart. But the one I was going to play stretched from California to New York, was almost *5000 miles* long, and would take 6-7 months to complete. At 39 years of age, doing it without a cart was not an option. The final element in golf is scoring. Most courses are rated as Par 72, meaning that a good golfer should complete the course in that many strokes, or swings. Also, each hole has an individual rating of 3, 4, or 5 based on difficulty and on how many strokes it should take to complete that hole. Simply put, the fewer strokes the better. Since no one had ever golfed across the United States, there was no established par, but Steve and I estimated that it would be around 200,000 strokes, give or take 50,000.

The plan was to tee off from Santa Monica Pier in southern California, and to make Hole #1 in Anaheim, some 40 miles away. And since I couldn't just sink a ball into any hole in Anaheim, or in any other city for that matter, I hired Southwest Greens, which is a company that installs regulation greens in backyards, to build one for me. Weston Weber, a teammate of mine with the Angels, owned the business and built greens in the first two cities of the tour for $3500 each, which was about half the usual price. His workers would go to the city where I was going to be, frame a 10x10-foot plywood box, and fill it with sand. They would tamp the sand, cover with Astroturf, and install a golf cup and flag, so that when I came down the road with a full set of clubs strapped onto my cart, there was an oasis in the middle of the desert. I'd hit the ball onto the green, putt two times, and that was it. But after spending $7000 on just two cities, it became too expensive, so Steve contacted officials from each city in advance and arranged for a central location for a symbolic finishing hole. Later, in Indianapolis, I suggested that we use the fountain in the center of the city. The city bought into the idea and placed two men in scuba gear in a large fountain holding the golf flag, while I chipped the ball in. I didn't know them, but they did it for the right reasons. I could never pay anyone to do that. It was a great idea and saved thousands of dollars.

The day before I arrived at a "Hole City," Steve would drive or fly in and meet with city officials to establish a route through the city and to address any logistical issues. Meanwhile, a semi-truck from EZ-Go would deliver spare golf cart tires and nine fresh carts to a designated fire station for my volunteer support crew and for the local police and fire department personnel to ride in. Once inside city limits, one volunteer would drive me in my cart, while two others would be in a cart ahead of me locating my ball and teeing up my next shot. To save time and to prevent me from chunking out pieces of asphalt and concrete from the streets with my iron clubs, we made makeshift tees by cutting foam rubber floor tile into six-inch squares and sticking a wood tee into them.

It takes a lot of balls to golf across the country, so Steve arranged a deal with Nike, but it ultimately fell through because of conflicts with us and Tiger Woods both using them. That was an easy choice for Nike, but Steve found a company in Chicago that made thousands of regulation golf balls for us with the *Golf Across The USA* logo stamped on them. I hit them across deserts, through prairies, and into any open space I could find. Normally, I would hit a ball 150-200 yards into someone's private acreage and play it from there, but if I couldn't get to it, I'd just drop another ball and continue swinging. There must be 10,000 golf balls lying around the freeways and buried in hundreds of cornfields across America.

Even Tiger Woods shanks, slices, and hooks a shot, so we knew that if I golfed down Main Street USA with real golf balls I would do serious damage to cars, pedestrians, storefronts, and windows, and end up broke, in jail, or both. Golf balls are extremely hard and have a bad effect on glass, automobiles, and human bone, but the solution was simple. When golfing in cities and through towns, I would hit a soft blue rubber handball. The United States Handball Association in Tucson donated hundreds of them to the tour, which we could pick up wherever we needed, saving significant money, but more importantly, the balls prevented scores of injuries, saved thousands of dollars in property damage, and kept me out of handcuffs. However, it took me until I got to El Paso to wise up and start using them. Before that, I literally putt-putted through several small towns holding my breath each time I mishit a ball or whenever the ball hopped and hit a rock or a crack in the road. There were a lot of anxious moments.

For transportation, I bought a used, white Ford F-250 pickup truck at the last minute, and Jerry Moyce, the owner of Swift Trucking in Phoenix, loaned me a 28-foot toy hauler to haul my two golf carts. It was exactly what I needed, but I had never driven a truck nor pulled anything that size before, and it would lead to quite an adventure later on. Once underway, the plan was for me to drive one golf cart, which held enough fuel for 95 miles, while a volunteer would drive the truck ahead 75-90 miles, detach the trailer, hook up the septic, then bring the truck back and bring water, food, or whatever I needed. If the cart broke down or had a flat, I would call the driver, but I would have to wait for him to unhook the trailer before he could come to me with tools. The goal each day was to cover at least 90 miles. At the end of most days, I stayed in a motel where I could shower, eat a good meal, and get a good night's rest.

The decision was made not to have the truck follow me with flashers on because it would bring more attention from the police. I preferred to risk being a tiny golf cart on the side of the road and not to be seen rather than having every highway patrolman spot me from two miles away. I drove in the pullout lane the whole way with no protection, and as people change tires or go across bridges, there was no room for me. I had a little mirror, but it shook, and I could never quite tell if someone was behind me. I also had to be careful in gauging the width of semi-trucks and wide loads. I almost got killed a hundred times a day. But when I left Phoenix, a guy from the Arizona Department of Transportation caught up with me outside Tucson

The ADOT man and my sign.

and gave me a large, yellow sign reading, "Caution – Charity Golfer Ahead," which I strapped to the back of my cart, so at least when someone came up on me from behind there was a large yellow sign warning them.

The most vital piece of equipment on my cart was the stereo system and CD player. Without it, and the Enya *The Memory of Trees* CD that I listened to everyday for almost seven months, the trip would have been impossible. That CD was the only thing that mellowed me out and protected others from my distinct version of golf cart road-rage.

Teeing Off

With months of mind-numbing preparation behind me, it was finally time to tee off. Everyone was excited and raring to go. Everyone except the city of Santa Monica. It appeared that the *Golf Across The USA* was off to ignominious start—if at all.

In the weeks leading to the event, we thought everything was set in stone. We had it on authority through the Santa Monica firefighters that I would be allowed to hit the ball up the beach and then cut in and go down the roads, and that later the police would escort me to the Anaheim Fire Station near Angels Stadium. But the day before I was to tee off, Steve visited the Director of Bays and Marinas, and she flatly refused to let me hit a golf ball down the beach. Steve countered that we had permission from the police, but she pointed out that a golf cart was unauthorized and that hitting a golf ball would be dangerous to people on the beach. Although Steve assured her than no one would be hit, she refused to budge and assured him that I would be stopped by the police. She informed him that I would be crossing through thirteen separate jurisdictions between Santa Monica and the place where we would be cutting inland, and that each beach city had its own police and fire departments, and that we had to get permission from each.

Time was running out. It was almost 3 o'clock in the afternoon on a Friday, and Steve was beginning to get physically ill, when he spotted a fire station and police station in nearby Manhattan Beach. He rolled the dice and drove to the police station and wrangled a meeting with the commander, who was guardedly sympathetic. When Steve explained our dilemma over jurisdiction and how we were denied permission to hit the ball on the beach, the chief had Steve call the director of bays and ask if she had jurisdiction over the sidewalk that runs down the beach. The director stated that she did not, but still refused to give us permission. Instead, she passed Steve on to another person, who said that they had never issued such a permit before. "How about now?" Steve asked boldly. The person then passed him on to two other people. Finally, Steve convinced one of the men to fax the permit application to him at a nearby Ralph's Grocery Store. He then received the unsigned permit, and was told that he had to come to Los Angeles in person to pay for it and to receive the signed copy. It was now past 4 o'clock, and it was physically impossible for him to get downtown in rush hour traffic. Steve then pulled a rabbit out of his hat and convinced the official, who told him that they had never waived a fee before, to make it a first time and to waive the fee on behalf of sick children. The man faxed the signed copy, and moments later, we were back in business.

With the permit finally obtained and all bureaucratic assess covered, I finally teed off from Santa Monica Pier and plowed my way to Anaheim, the home of Disneyland and the Angels. I recall the mixed bag of emotions I carried; frustration with the bureaucracy of government; disgust with the media for what I viewed as a relative lack of interest in bringing attention to afflicted children; and confusion with the seeming indifference that so many people harbored to the cause that I embraced. But with that first swing, all negativity, like the ball from my club, sailed into the warm morning sun and reminded that sick children everywhere were bravely fighting for their lives, waiting for me to rescue them, because that's what firefighters do.

Santa Monica Pier and Golf Across The USA Tour.

I teed off from a little league field in Anaheim and golfed down the side of the freeway to Hole #2 in Las Vegas, some 265 miles to the east, only to get stuck in deep mud some 40 miles away. Fortunately, it was early in the year and was not yet 130 degrees in the shade. That would come later. A few miles outside of the city, police and firefighters stopped traffic as I hit a regulation golf ball down the Strip accompanied by an Elvis impersonator, passing the iconic Las Vegas sign and the Mandalay Bay Hotel & Casino on my left. A little farther and I was downtown hitting a ball through the Aladdin Casino, out the back door, and through a residential neighborhood. Golfing through Las Vegas was a thrill. I especially loved the non-stop movement and the lure of the casinos and their garish neon lights pulling people in, taking their money, and pushing them down the strip to the next lucky spot. I did stay for one night, and fortunately, I held on to my money. However, I wasn't so lucky with my first cart. It only made it to two holes, but the next one made it all the way to New York City. Despite several flat tires, it never broke down.

Even in Las Vegas you don't see this everyday.

Hoover Dam

The Hoover Dam doesn't shut down for anyone— or so I was told. As a national landmark and a major source of energy in the West and Southwest, the Hoover Dam area is a busy place. Traffic moving eastward and westward on the narrow old US Highway 93 winds through the Black Mountains like a giant snake threatening to devour everything in its path, but the traffic had no way of knowing that the Hoover Dam was going to my personal tee box for Hole #3 on the *Golf Across The USA* Tour. My goal was to convince the government that they should stop traffic both ways for 30 minutes on one of the busiest highways in the region and to allow me to hit a symbolic ball some 400 yards across the dam. To me the logic was undeniable, but the authorities needed proof.

My audition shot.

A few weeks prior to the planned tee off, I had been refused permission to even try because no one at the dam believed I could do it anyway. Excuse me! They were messing with the same person who once attempted to break the world pogo stick jumping record. Steve and I boldly drove to the Bureau of Reclamation and met with a woman whom we convinced to make a few phone calls on my behalf. The visit essentially earned me a tryout at the helipad with the site director.

"You can hit all the balls you want from here. A lot have tried, but no one has ever done it. If you hit the other side of the canyon wall at eye level, I'll shut down traffic and let you hit across the dam."

Since I still had some time before the tour, I trained, worked out, and got myself into shape. When the day arrived to audition, I came through. After about ten balls, I launched one that hit the canyon wall above eye

What a Hoover Dam nice shot!

level, and that was all that the director needed to see. He shut down traffic in the entire canyon for 20 minutes while I hit balls from a tee-box that the firefighters had built at the visitor's center across the dam. No permits. No fees. Nothing. The people at the dam allowed me to do it because they believed in what I was doing, and they saw that I was honest, dedicated, and passionate about my cause. They were right.

With a huge notch in my belt, I got on my golf cart, drove to the other side of Hoover Dam, and chipped the ball down the side of the freeway until I got to Wickenburg, Arizona. From there, I went south to my home base of Glendale to Hole #3, where I received a great reception. My fellow firefighters even turned out en masse and constructed a nice green for me to putt on. Without the support of the fire chief, union president, and the scores of men who covered my shifts, the tour would have been impossible. Thanks guys.

Glendale Police & Fire welcome Steve and me home.

Hole #4

The rumor was that the grounds crew at Bank One Ballpark in Phoenix, now called Chase Field, the home of the Arizona Diamondbacks Baseball Team, didn't think I could hit a golf ball up and over the stadium from home plate. The gauntlet had been thrown down, and I was eager to respond. I'm so competitive that telling me that I can't do something is tantamount to declaring war on me, and that was just the motivation I needed. With my daughter Lauren, and my son David, with me at the park, I launched a ball out of the stadium on my tee-off to Hole #4 in El Paso, Texas. Several police officers had shut down traffic outside the stadium while others chased the ball down the street once it landed. It was one of the most gratifying golf shots of the entire tour. Tell me I can't do something, especially when in my mind every shot helps a child who is sick and struggling for their life.

Bank One Ball Park.

A Little Help from My Friends

People sometimes amaze me. On the way home from Hoover Dam, I stopped at a sandwich shop outside of Kingman, Arizona, to have lunch. I parked my golf cart in front of the shop, and as I was inside eating, a woman walks in and says, "Oh my God, are you a firefighter? My husband would love this!"

Her husband, Gene Stafford, who was a retired firefighter with multiple sclerosis, was eager to help, which was lucky for me, since I was traveling with a 71-year-old retired General Motors employee by the name of Ron Wojcik, who had only committed to travel with me for my first 30 days. Normally, I wanted a person to commit to me to 3-6 weeks, but that seldom happened due to personal emergencies, family commitments, health problems, and other reasons. However, this guy was awesome. He had outstanding skills and helped build and operate my website from the command trailer. He committed to travel with me for eight weeks and joined me after El Paso, Texas, but the tour ultimately became so stressful, that his MS flared up and he started to go blind in one eye. He kept going to the hospital and taking antibiotics, but when we eventually got to St. Louis, Missouri it got so bad that he just disappeared in the middle of the night. One minute I was sitting in a hotel with a driver, and the next minute he was gone. So, I called my contact at my next stop in Evansville, Indiana, and told him that I didn't know how I would get the other carts there without a driver for my truck and trailer, but that I could get my cart there. But that wasn't the problem. I was delayed for two days until one of Evansville's firefighters committed to helping me. Throughout the tour as I would get a person to drive, I would always be thinking about the next. *Who can I meet? Who can I call? Is this guy going to last!* And as I got closer to the end of the tour, I got more nervous, so I would convince a fire department to supply one of their men for a few weeks, or I would simply meet a guy on the side of the highway to go with me. Either way, it was all good. I want to thank Wally Monsivaiz, Ron Wajak, Robbie Doerr, Ron MacKnight, Keith Kanner, Gene Stafford, and Ron Miller for their support on the tour. They helped make it fun.

Desert Fun

I live in a desert and I am used to the heat. But spending all day, every day, driving along a scorched highway golfing under a blistering sun is not for the weak, timid, or pale. In the Phoenix area, temperatures often exceed 90 degrees in the spring and over 110 degrees in the summer, and people almost lose their minds because of the oppressive and unrelenting heat. True, it's a dry heat—but so is an oven! That is why I scheduled to golf the hotter regions of the southwest in the early spring and to move east with the passing summer.

After leaving Phoenix, it was off to El Paso, which was the beginning of a searing, six-week odyssey across the Lone Star State that tested my endurance, my commitment, and at times, my sanity. It was so hot in El Paso that the firefighters there were so concerned that I wasn't going to make it alone, that they modified my golf cart. It was 140 degrees on the highway, so they went to Home Depot and bought tubing and installed a customized misting system all around the top of my golf cart and connected it to a large bug spray canister that they filled with ice. When I got hot, I pumped the sprayer and opened the petcock valve and it misted me while I was driving down the highway.

The firefighters were also afraid that I wouldn't make it to Van Horn, which was only about 90 miles away, that they wouldn't let me start until they had taken me past an exit more than five miles outside of town. They figured that the reduction in distance would provide a buffer that might just save my life. To compound their fears, my driver at the time was a 71-year-old man with emphysema that I met at a Starbucks in Arizona. Heat was the least of my worries.

Remember the Alamo!

South of the Border

My desire to hit a golf ball from Mexico across the Rio Grande River back into the United States almost got me thrown into jail. Steve and I, along with my drivers, left El Paso with two golf carts and wanted to travel south to the All-American Bridge and cross into Juarez, Mexico, where we would meet our fellow

Mexican firefighters, known as *Bomberos*, and travel to the town square for a celebration.

As usual, Steve was on point and went on ahead into Juarez to find a mariachi band to play at the tee-off, but when I got to the entry point, the border official would not let me in with my golf carts. I tried to contact Steve, but he was out of range of my cell phone, so I remained there trying to convince the official that I was not going to sell "black market golf carts" in Mexico, which apparently he was concerned about. The *Bomberos* came to my aid and tried to help, but the official become more agitated. Finally, I reached Steve on my phone, and saw him and a television cameraman about 200 yards away walking toward the entry point. Steve stopped about every fifty yards, waved his hands, and pointed toward me like he was directing the cameraman to film me being detained. But it was only a ruse to force the official into letting me in. They filmed all the way up to the point of entry, which further infuriated the official. Steve arrived and spoke sternly to him, "Do you realize that you're probably causing an international incident?" The official stared at him. "What do you mean?" Steve didn't blink.

"We filmed the whole thing. Television in the U.S. and in Mexico is going to show that you were the man who wrongly refused to allow Dave Graybill to cross the border and kept him from raising money for sick children. Do you want to be that man?"

The official pointed to the thick book in his other hand and repeatedly cited regulations. Finally, Steve had enough. "I called people and arranged this!" he shouted. The official shouted back, "Who did you call?"

Steve confidently took out his address book and began stating the names of people he knew in the capital, Mexico City. He then asked, "And what is your name so I can tell them you are the man that who would not allow us to come into the country?"

Photo op with the Juarez Bomberos.

The Mexican official was a large man, and he was sweating profusely. He then ordered the cameramen to stop filming and to put their cameras down, but Steve told him that we already had enough film to make our case and restated that he would be calling "some important people." The official grew worried and finally wrote down the serial numbers of our two golf carts. He then made me sign a handwritten paper stating that I would return with the carts through this port of entry within a certain time frame. I quickly signed the paper and rode triumphantly into Juarez armed with 200 dozen donuts. After a brief celebration, I teed up a ball and drove it across the Rio Grande River onto a high school football field in Texas. Adios Mexico!

How bout' them Cowboys

In the late 1970s and early 80s, "Dallas" was the most popular show on television. Each week millions of people watched the rich and powerful Ewing family build its financial empire from their sprawling South Fork Ranch. Almost 20 years later, I rolled into Dallas looking to build a fortune for children's charities. Little did I know that South Fork would be the site of our largest crowd, albeit somewhat by default, because over 150,000 people were there attending a Christian music festival. But a captive audience was better than no audience, and the raucous crowd cheered wildly as I chipped a ball up on a stage and putted out.

A Close Call

Two months into the tour, as we were leaving Texas for Oklahoma City, we ran into a 30-mile stretch of highway construction that prevented me from driving my cart and hitting any golf balls, and since I was unable to drive my cart, I took the opportunity to drive the truck. We quickly loaded the cart and entered the construction zone. Since I had no experience pulling a large, heavy trailer with an elaborate hitch and brake system, I was bound to mess up. I forgot to insert the safety pin in the hitch, and although I had chained it, I had not secured the pin that locks the hitch in place. As I was speeding along the bumpy road about ten miles inside Oklahoma talking with Steve on the phone, I heard a loud bang and felt a strong jolt. To my horror, the trailer had come off the hitch and we were pulling it by only two small safety chains. Suddenly, the truck fishtails uncontrollably and semi trucks in front of us begin pulling off the road preparing for an accident. The truck then jackknifes, breaking the safety chains, and sending us in a full circle spin. Meanwhile, the trailer is rolling down the freeway at 50 miles per hour before veering off and crashing through a fence into a huge pasture dotted with cows. The cows started spilling through the fence onto the road and the freeway had to be shut down. We sat in a ditch while the trailer rested upright in the field a quarter mile away. If there was ever a time to quit, this was it. Steve recalls the accident:

My runaway trailer.

"One afternoon I was talking to Dave on the phone and I hear tires screeching, and Dave said in a deadpan fashion, 'I've got to hang up

now. We're going to have an accident.' I kept the phone on, but he threw his phone down and I could hear all the stuff flying around in the truck, and then there was silence. After a few moments, I heard stirring in the truck cab, and then Dave picked up the phone. 'Are you still there?' 'I'm here,' I replied. 'What happened?' Dave was more animated this time. 'We just had a wreck. But we're okay!' It was miraculous that no one was killed. But Dave is one of those people who steps in crap and his shoes come out clean."

Steve was right. I was lucky. As I sat buckled in the truck waiting for help, I thought about the sick children who needed the money I was generating, and about the promises I had made to a lot of good people who had sacrificed and supported me on the tour. Physically, I was not injured. Although my ego was bruised and I suffered from a momentary bout of self-pity, I decided that nothing was going to stop me from getting to NYC and finishing what I started. It's ironic, but once I told the police, the fire rescue people, the farmers, and everyone else that arrived, the story of what I was doing and why, the whole county seemed to come together. The police didn't give me a ticket. The firefighters pulled the trailer out of the field and took us to the next town 25 miles away. And the farmers mended the fence for free. The next morning we went to a Home Depot, and Gene Stafford, one of the guys who was traveling with me at the time, fixed the plumbing underneath the trailer, and within four hours, we were on our way. We were lucky we didn't die and lucky that the *Golf Across The USA Tour* was able to continue. The generosity and kindness of so many kind people in southern Oklahoma proved to me that the biggest hearts weren't just in Texas.

The Beat Goes on

The near fatal accident made me pine for normalcy and quiet. I found it in the Midwest. As I moved eastward, the cities were closer together, and if the people there couldn't give me money, they fed me. The compassion and kindness I received was unbelievable. I didn't ask for a lot, but if they wanted to acknowledge what I was doing with a hug and a piece of food, God bless them. Life is simple.

Firefighters in Kansas City.

In rapid succession, the tour stopped in Oklahoma City, Kansas City, and St. Louis. In Kansas City, I teed off from beautiful Royals Park and sank my ball into the right center field fountain on the first try, for which the stadium people set off an awesome fireworks display.

But in St. Louis, the park district refused to let me hit a ball from the top of the famous 630-foot Gateway

Arch. I suggested that I they let me take an elevator to the top and to use a service hatch to gain entrance to the outside where someone would secure me atop the arch by a harness and straps. Once in place, I would drive a golf ball into the nearby Mississippi River. Despite my best efforts, St. Louis wouldn't buy into my plan and I left mumbling that Missouri didn't deserve its *Show Me State* moniker.

Playing through in St. Louis.

I concluded the front nine of the Golf Across The USA Tour in Louisville, Kentucky, where I golfed down the home stretch at historic Churchill Downs, home of the Kentucky Derby. Being half-finished with anything is significant because it's an emotional shot in the arm and a huge confidence boost. But being half-finished also means being half unfinished, and that motivated me even more. After all, I had been a closer, and closers like to finish.

The gang at Churchill Downs.

"Tanks" for the memories in Columbus, Indiana.

The Back Nine

After a few quick stops in Indiana, I planned to blow smoothly into the Windy City, but on a busy stretch of Interstate 65 outside of Harvey, Illinois, I was reminded that even the "best laid plans of mice and men often go awry." Four police cars quickly surrounded my golf cart expecting to find a lunatic. The officer in charge thought I was a nut and threatened to take me in to have me evaluated. "You can't do this," he said. "There is no way this is legal. You can't be whacking golf balls along one of the busiest highways in the country."

Apparently, he hadn't heard of me. "Do you know who I am?" I asked sternly. "I really don't give a damn," he replied. "You still can't do it."

I then handed him a brochure. "I'm a firefighter supported by the Fraternal Order of Police, the National Association of Police Officers, and by every police organization in the country in service to kids who are sitting in a hospital room getting ready to die. Tell me I can't golf here!"

"I didn't know," he said. I sensed an opportunity to attack. "I know you don't know. But do you know how hard it is for every station to let their patrolman know to let me golf through their community? I'm sorry you didn't get the message, but if you hit a golf ball, you'll let everyone see that policeman truly care about kids. Try the seven-iron."

To my surprise, the officer smiled, adjusted his hat, and pulled up his trousers. "Give me a club," he said wryly, as cars whizzed by with several patrol cars parked in the median and all around my cart. The officer then teed up a ball on the side of the freeway, did a couple of rear end waggles, then ripped the ball into a cornfield. Trucker sped past blowing their air horns and everyone smiled. It was one of the most unforgettable moments of the tour. The officer then led us through miles of construction to the Harvey Fire Station, where a group of surprised firefighters met us. "What are you doing here?" they exclaimed. "No one comes to Harvey. We have the highest crime rate in the country. If you had any idea of what you were doing, you'd never come here."

Hanging out in Harvey.

I just told them that I was there to get a little love and that it was one of my best stops. They responded with hospitality. The men of the fire station washed and fueled my cart, fed us a lasagna dinner, and put us up for the night. The Harvey guys were wonderful and it was quite an adventure. Whenever I think of Harvey, I fondly recall the highway patrolman making me promise that if he hit a ball he would never appear on the evening news. Taken literally, being in a book is not being on the news. Not yet, anyway.

The guys at Harvey feeding me!

Chicago—My Kind of Town

I never hit a golf ball from the Sears Tower in Chicago, but I got to do the next best thing—acting like I was and getting a photo taken while doing it. Like always, Steve Kolesar was terrific on the phone and convinced the people at the Sears Tower to allow me and my entourage, which also included my children, to stage a shot on an open-air, L-shaped observation deck on the 95th floor of the building. It was cold and sleeting when we got up there, and I began taking full practice swings at a plastic Cayman ball while our photographer set up the ladder and camera. I was intentionally just missing the ball with my practice swings, and the man assigned to us became stressed out. He feared that the club might slip out of my hands or that the ball might accidentally drop off the edge of the building and kill someone on the ground. But we were allowed to do our thing, and given the security still in place after 9-11, that in itself was a minor miracle.

Although hitting a ball into the Buckingham Fountain and launching a symbolic tee shot from the Sears Tower were highlights of the stop, spending time with my kids in Chicago was special. Nothing compared to

The Sears Tower overlooking Lake Michigan.

having them with me at the photo shoot at the Sears Tower and in sharing the joy and wonder of doing something selfless for children less fortunate. I hope they always remember how much great Chicago style pizza we ate and how much fun we had together on that trip.

The next leg of the tour was in Michigan. I made stops in the Detroit area, and in Battle Creek, where I teed off from the famous Kellogg's cereal sign next to Tony the Tiger. I followed that with a lap of golfing around the Michigan International Raceway in Brooklyn. From there I traveled to the Cleveland area, and then to Pittsburgh, before concluding my trip in cities along the Eastern seaboard.

Starting my engine at the Michigan Speedway.

The people in the upper Midwest and Ohio Valley were among the finest I had met anywhere, and I was amazed at their resiliency despite the trying economic conditions that they faced, particularly in Detroit, Cleveland, and Pittsburgh. To see the once mighty factories of three of America's great industrial cities in steep decline and rampant decay was a sad testament to the condition of our nation as producer. To have fallen so fast and to such depths weighed heavily on me, especially in Pennsylvania, my father's home state. Golfing through the streets of Pittsburgh was not easy, but thanks to Jim Flaherty, Local Union #1, and to all their firefighters, we made a lasting impact on the citizens of the Steel City. One of the goals that Steve and I set was to hit a golf ball out of as many major league ballparks as possible, including gorgeous PNC Park in Pittsburgh, which we did.

Hitting this shot was grrrrrrreat!! That's me to the right of the TM below the C.

Catch me Mr. President

I relate everything to the game of baseball, and one of my dreams has always been to play catch with the President of the United States. Everywhere I went on the *Golf Across The USA* Tour, I carried two baseball gloves and a ball with me in my cart in the event that someone wanted to play catch. Prior to driving my golf cart through Washington, DC, we contacted The White

House stating my desire to play catch with President George W. Bush. Following 9-11, it was my hope to meet him, to have him give me an acknowledgment of a job well done, and then to play catch. And although

PNC Park in Pittsburg.

it didn't happen, my visit to the nation's capital was unforgettable. Somehow, Steve wrangled permission for me to golf through the National Mall, but as I was hitting from the Lincoln Memorial, he took a photo that almost got us into trouble. Since no one is allowed to use monuments to promote anything, Steve and I almost went to jail, but we talked the police out of it. It was quite the scene, me hitting golf balls with the statue of Lincoln looming in the background and a swarm of Japanese tourists perched on the steps shooting photos of me, while hundreds of kids out in the landing area were catching my blue handballs. Afterwards, I got out of town and made stops at Oriole's Park in Baltimore, and near the Liberty Bell in Philadelphia, before moving on to Hole #18 in New York City, the final stop on the *Golf Across The USA* Tour.

Mr. Lincoln, mind if I play through?

Outside the Capitol Building in DC.

A Hole in One

During my stop in Philadelphia, I told several people that I planned to drive north to New Jersey, through the Lincoln Tunnel, and into New York City, and that I was going to conclude the tour by hitting a golf ball in Central Park.

"You can't golf through NYC," they responded. "Too much traffic. Can't be done. No way!"

I had just spent six-and-a-half months golfing from the Pacific Ocean, across the Hoover Dam, into Chicago, up to Detroit, over to Washington, DC, and past the Liberty Bell, and people were still telling me I couldn't go through NYC. "It's not Mars," I countered, "It's just another place with another group of people living in it." So much for the City of Brotherly Love.

But the Big Apple was everything I hoped it would be and the highlight of the tour. I basked in a triumphant entrance into one of the world's great cities signaling the symbolic and real end to the most difficult and rewarding thing I had ever done. Sadly, I didn't want it to end.

An hour before I teed off, Steve had everything arranged. Extra golf carts were lined up along Times Square and the NYPD was out in full force waiting to escort me the 14 miles into the city. Some of the firefighters that I had met and who had supported me on the golf tour, had flown in and were allowed to ride in the extra golf carts. Other volunteers rode along and filmed the event. After spending nearly seven months in a golf cart on the side of a freeway on my own time and with my own money on behalf of sick children, I had envisioned that the NYC Fire Department and thousands of citizens would be lining the streets and that they would treat me to an overwhelming, euphoric finish. It was euphoric all right, but the firefighters were noticeable absent. Many of my brothers in uniform will swear that they didn't get the memo or that they didn't know about it, while others will say that they simply didn't care. And that's okay.

But the NYC Police Department was there. And not because 300 boxes of Krispy Kreme Doughnuts were on hand. One police officer, who looked like the good black cop in the first *Die Hard* movie, was sitting on a scooter in Times Square when I arrived to tee off. He had something to say:

> *"Dave, I'm your guide today, and you have no idea what this means. I got to work this morning and got a personal briefing from my chief and my sergeant, who never show up to briefings, and they said that there was a firefighter coming to the city to hit a golf ball for sick children. He's been on the road for several months, and he's teeing off from Times Square and running a 14-mile route through the city into Central Park. If that guy wants to hit a golf ball on the sidewalk, through a building, into a bank, over a bus, anywhere he wants to hit a ball, you let him hit a ball."*

He added that he had never been to a briefing where there were no rules for an event and that he wanted to have some fun. I couldn't let him down.

One of coolest things was that the NYC police officers, who are under total control and heavy scrutiny, were told they could do whatever they wanted by allowing a guy to hit a ball through the streets. They had a blast weaving in and out of traffic on their scooters, driving up on sidewalks, and doing figure eights around parking meters. They allowed me to hit the ball off the tops of buses and awnings, and to bounce them off people and cars without so much as a frown. The police enjoyed themselves so much because they were allowed to be ordinary people, and they thanked me for it. When the police have fun, everybody has fun.

Finally, after about two hours in the city, I hit one last ball into a flagpole base in Central Park. Abruptly, *Golf Across The USA* was over after 142,800 shots, leaving me with an overwhelming sense of what to do next. I was a high-adrenaline, results-oriented guy who was now without a cause or an enemy to fight. But first, it was time to heal.

Tackling the Big Apple on the Golf Across The USA Tour.

Aftermath

Because of legal liability, permits, money, and scores of other obstacles, it is unlikely that anything like the *Golf Across The USA Tour* will ever be done again in this country. It was a unique and unbelievably rewarding experience, but I consider it a failure. Although my intentions were good and I had a strong desire to help people, too much focus was on me hitting the ball and not enough on the thousands of children suffering with cancer. Although we didn't have the right avenue of support or a direct pipeline to get the money to help the kids, we did raise $150,000 through one sponsor. But the sponsors were also part of the problem.

All that my sponsors seemed to care about was if people were donating money. "Why aren't people donating money?" they would ask. "Why aren't you on TV and why aren't you on the national news?" Not only did I have to golf, I had to arrange the marketing and PR for the sponsors. Sure, they gave me in-kind donations, but even while I was golfing, they were pressuring me saying that I wasn't putting them on the news. I told EZ-Go, "I just went through 38 cities with nine EZ-Go golf carts with your big sign on the side of them. I don't know what that registers in marketing dollars, but I shut down New York City and the people saw nine EZ-Go golf carts peppering people with golf balls. What do you want?"

Their answer was clear. Just before I got back to Arizona, EZ-Go wanted my golf cart that had all the decals and patches from police and fire departments across the country plastered all over it. I didn't care about the other carts, but that cart was the one that every firefighter sat in and the one that went through every city. When I got home. I hid it from EZ-Go, moving it from one friend's house to another. Ultimately, I had to give it back. "Can't you just give me the cart," I asked. "After seven months, I think I earned it."

However, the corporate game has its own rules, and they must be followed. But if one goes corporate, they die. I gained 15 pounds during the tour and was stressed out all the time. All we did was eat. PF Changs hosted parties everywhere we went, and Krispy Kreme provided doughnuts at every stop, and by the time the tour was over we were foundered on Chinese food and doughnuts. Not only do corporate sponsors want their stuff back, they try to kill you slowly while they are doing it! From this point on, no more sponsors. More about that later.

Lessons learned

The greatest lesson that I learned from the *Golf Across The USA* Tour was that I could come up with an idea, put it into action, and see it through. I also learned that regardless of how intelligent, how educated, how independent, how competitive, or how motivated a person, they cannot do everything by themselves. Creating a team for success is vital. But in the final analysis, inspiration is still the single most important element of success. Without a dream, there is no action. And without action, there is no realizing the dream. It's a simplistic formula with a valid approach at its core, and it has served me well. I hope that the through the *Golf Across The USA* Tour I helped some sick kids and showed some people that they can accomplish anything if they believe in it enough, are willing to work hard, and dare to dream big.

CHAPTER 3
GUARDIANS OF THE RIBBON

Five years had passed since the *Golf Across The USA Tour* and I was bored. Since sinking that final shot on the 18th green in Central Park in New York City, I had settled into the routine of life. A divorced father of two. Former minor league baseball player. Employee number 06310, firefighter for the city of Glendale. *Is this all there is?* I wondered. *Is this my legacy?*

I knew that the moment I retired from the fire department I would be forgotten, and that another employee and another employee number would take my place. Like countless others before me, I would limp off into the sunset and live out the rest of my life drawing a meager pension, simply waiting to die in my own little retirement village. It's not how a man should go out and it wasn't how I wanted to be remembered, so I began thinking of ways of setting an example and raising the bar for myself. But I realized that in America, unless you can buy popularity, have been gifted with a talent, or have the marketing behind you to sell something tangible that people can make money off of you, it's hard to raise the bar. You have to make your own bar, and then jump over it in a profound and unique way, like *Golfing Across The USA*. But that isn't easy either, because the national media rarely spends much time or energy covering the philanthropic efforts of the common man. Disaster and scandal make headlines and drive ratings, and getting the word out about feel-good efforts is difficult without the long, hairy arm of the national media supporting it. They would rather devote air time to sex scandals, crime, and celebrity gossip, rather than advancing stories that inspire people to get out and to help others.

Employee #06310.

Cares Enough to Wear Pink

Early in the summer of 2007, Wally Monsivaiz, a firefighter from Las Cruces, New Mexico whom I had met on the way to El Paso on the Golf Across The USA Tour, called me at the station. It had been four years since we had last spoken, but Wally wanted to let me know that the Las Cruces Fire Department came up with an idea to wear pink shirts to help women with breast cancer, and that they were helping a for-profit organization called *Tough Enough to Wear Pink*. He wanted to know if I liked the idea, and if our department might be interested in joining. Initially, I thought it was a good idea, but I didn't commit. First, I needed the advice of someone I valued and loved.

Lisa and I popped the cork on a $7 bottle of red merlot and went to work discussing the merits of Wally's offer. While I thought it was a worthwhile organization, I did not want to work for it nor get involved. I was sick of tax-based organizations like firefighters, policemen, and teachers being recruited or made to work for other organizations. Why can't we own our own? Why can't blue collar workers and common citizens create and own a program that serves communities? For me, it was time to put the power in the hands of those who bore the weight of the work. Second, I didn't like the name. *Tough Enough to Wear Pink* had to go. Being tough had nothing to do with wearing the color pink, but caring did, and that's when I decided on *Cares Enough to Wear Pink*. Pink represents women, and people have to care enough to wear pink in support of women and their battles. Not just against cancer, but against anything that threatens them. We had another glass of wine, and then we began firing off ideas. We went on the internet to see if *Cares Enough to Wear Pink* had been used. It had not, and we knew we had something good. Lisa recalls the event:

> *"I remember thinking what a great idea! And I knew that Dave would turn it into something amazing that the whole country could support and that he would carry it through. That's what makes Dave so different than anybody else. He*

is both the most exasperating and amazing man that I've ever known. He is just infectious. He's great to talk to; great to listen to; and great to watch tell stories. He's extremely funny and I love to be made to laugh. When I first met him he was gregarious and joyful and extremely positive. From the moment I met him he didn't badger me with trying to take me out to dinner. Our first encounter was over coffee in a coffee shop, and I walked away knowing that I had met someone special. Then we went to dinner, and I've been smitten ever since. Our first date was on Valentine's Day 2004. He invited me to be his guest at an awards dinner where he received the American Red Cross Real Hero Award. If that doesn't win a girl over, I don't know what does."

I woke the following morning with a boilerplate churning in my head and it was exploding with ideas. Being true to my hyperactive nature, I threw myself into the work of creating an organization built on love and hope. I jotted down ideas, made plans, and got advice from family and friends, and from people I knew who would not support me. Repeat—from people who *WOULD NOT* support me. Doubt, negativity, and conflict had always fueled me and inspired me to wage war, so I took the idea and created an LLC and registered the name *Guardians of the Ribbon, Inc.*, which represents that we, as people, protect different awareness ribbons that are used all over the country for women's causes. But when people hear or see *Guardians of the Ribbon*, they assume that the organization only represents breast cancer, which is not true. It represents all women, but specifically those battling cancer.

It was then that I came up with the crazy idea of building a huge stainless steel ribbon called the

The first Guardians of the Ribbon.

Ribbon of Hope. It would be mounted on a pink trailer and pulled behind a pink fire truck to different events in support of women. In my thinking, the ribbon had to be stainless steel, because stainless steel doesn't rust, and "as stainless steel never ages, our endearing love for our women will never change. Those of us who haven't been affected standing up for those who have." This motto symbolized an endearing and pure love for the women we would represent. Also, I wanted to capture the hearts of hardworking people. Like any memorial or monument that represents or acknowledges an ideal, event, or person, I wanted the ribbon to represent the love, passion, and labor that it took to build it and to serve as a reminder of our need and responsibility to make a difference. I wanted a fire truck because I was a firefighter and because it represented the hope and rescue that we're all about.

With the idea fresh in my head, I drove directly to Maricopa Metals, the company that had just finished building my home, and I asked the owner to build a 10-foot, 4000-pound statue of a ribbon from stainless steel. The owners believed in me and in what I was doing, so they paid for all the stainless steel and for almost 700 hours of labor by Johnny Salmeron and Leo Balcazar, who did an excellent job constructing it. This included the hiring of a Hungarian craftsman to finish it. The statue is also a fountain. I had it plumbed in copper and had a small trough cut in the top so that water could run down over it. All it needed to become functional was to have the pump hooked up, and for a water source to be installed. My goal was that once it had traveled the country for 15 or 20 years, and once it had touched millions of lives, it would be permanently planted somewhere as a tribute to women.

That next spring, the ribbon was finished and was mounted on a trailer donated by Steve Cannon, a fellow firefighter. The trailer was modified and balanced to the statue so it would roll down the road straight. Finally, the trailer was painted and the statue dedicated on April 23, 2008. More than three years later, it still shines as a Ribbon of Hope.

"I met Dave Graybill in April of 2008, at the funeral of my niece, who passed away at age 38 from breast cancer. Dave was there at the request of a fellow firefighter, and that day he

brought the only piece of equipment he had – a beautiful stainless steel ribbon on a pink trailer. Dave didn't just bring a ribbon that day, he brought a dream. He told me he was going to build a fleet of pink fire trucks to travel all over the country to honor women battling cancer. Indeed, he has made that dream a reality."
~Debbie Schmidt

Stainless steel Ribbon of Hope.

Trial by Fire Department

Now that I had the perfect program, I had to convince the Glendale Fire Department and my firefighters union to wear pink tee shirts. It was easier said than done.

The firefighters union constantly works to help the community and it expects its firefighters to pitch in. Since I did not participate in many union events, I rarely went to meetings, but knowing that my fire chief didn't like me and that attending one would give me an ideal opportunity to reach about 200 peers in the fire service, I went to explain my *Cares Enough to Wear Pink* idea. For added effect, I had a pink shirt made that read, *Glendale Fire Department Cares Enough to Wear Pink*, and I brought it to the meeting. When it came my turn to speak, I stood and gave my spiel to the fire chief, the union president, and to the other firefighters. I explained that we would be one of the first fire departments in the country to wear pink shirts and to have our own slogan, and that I would get a fire truck, paint it pink, and drive it across America to inspire other communities to raise money to battle cancer. I had intentionally put my chief on the spot, and he knew it. He realized that Chrystal Sorenson, a firefighter who had recently been diagnosed with breast cancer, and who had also undergone a mastectomy, was in attendance, and that not publicly backing such a program would be unpopular. He quickly acknowledged that it was a great idea and that he would support it if he could get the city manager on board. "Run with it," he said. Famous last words.

Armed with a verbal acknowledgment from the chief given in front of 200 peers, I was hopeful that the city manager would give his approval, which was necessary for the plan to go through. I walked out of the meeting feeling confident that I would soon have the full support of the Glendale Fire Department and the city. But in the event that I did not get approval, I already had a backup plan. I was going to acquire my own pink fire truck, travel across the country on my time if necessary, and make a difference in the lives of people everywhere, whether the department or the city liked it or not.

The men of the Glendale Fire Department were scheduled to wear their *Cares Enough to Wear Pink* shirts on October 25, 2007, but in the weeks and days leading up to the date, the fire chief had not called me back with the okay. He kept saying that he was waiting to meet with the city manager, but in my mind, both he and the city manager were blowing me off, and although I was frustrated at being put on hold, I welcomed the conflict that was brewing. I would not be put off, and I would not go away quietly. Both the fire chief and the union president told me to go ahead and to have shirts made for every firefighter, and since I didn't want anyone using the excuse that they didn't have any money, I sized each and every person on the fire department, purchased the pink tee shirts with my own money, and personally applied the logos. Then I hand delivered the 250 shirts, each according to size, to each person on the fire department. It took two weeks to make the shirts and another five days to deliver them. With the shirts distributed by early October, word was still not received from the city manager, and I began to sweat. I pressed the fire chief for an answer, but he kept saying that he still hadn't received permission from the city manager. Finally, the day before we were supposed to wear our shirts, I called the fire chief. His secretary delivered the message that the city manager did not want the firefighters to wear the shirts, because if he allowed them to do it, he would have to allow all city employees to do it, and that wouldn't be fair. When the firefighters heard that the city manager denied the request, about half threw their shirts in the trash. That's when my conflict with the fire chief and city manager began.

I immediately sidestepped my chief and called Mayor Elaine Scruggs, who I consider a true leader and an angel on earth. I couldn't believe that all this was happening and that she hadn't heard about it. "There is no way this could be kept secret," I chided. "I can't believe the city of Glendale would do this! This is crap!"

"Excuse me," said Elaine. "Calm down. I do not know what you are talking about. Tell me what is wrong."

I was floored. It was obvious that she did not know and had not been informed of my program or my request to the city manager, so I proceed to tell her. To her credit, she listened patiently for several minutes. Finally, she spoke:

> *"Dave, I know you, and if your heart is in the right place, and if you're doing this selflessly, you're probably going to feel some resistance, but if you need to help people, go for it."*

Apparently, the fire chief was angry because I went out of the chain of command by calling the city manager, and then the mayor. True, I went out of the chain of command, but I was tired of the chain of command squashing good ideas, especially when the ideas were forward thinking and aimed at helping others with no cost to the city. The city manager said that he had no idea what had happened, but I soon discovered that the fire chief had kept the shirts under his desk and had not gone to the city manager, then used the city manager as the scapegoat as to why we couldn't do it. When I confronted the fire chief and caught him in a lie, he dug in and said that he didn't care if it made Glendale firefighters look good or not, he was never going to let them wear pink shirts.

The Phoenix Fire Department wasn't much better. The fire chief had told me that if I came up with an idea to create PR for the fire department, or to do good things in community, to call him, so I went to him and he loved the idea. I thought Phoenix was going to help me, but they didn't want to get in the way because I was a City of Glendale employee, which would create problems. Phoenix used the "We're in a budget crisis, so we can't ask the firefighters to wear pink shirts" excuse. Afterwards, I thought it better to slay the head of the dragon instead of the tail.

One week later, *Guardians of the Ribbon* was incorporated as a 501(c)(3) non-profit charitable organization. The name itself implied a dedicated group of noble men united in a romantic crusade against the enemies of women—namely, cancer. But in reality, Lisa and I were the corporation. At this time, all we had were grand ideas of launching a nationwide tour to raise money to fight cancer. We didn't have a completed ribbon, nor did we have a pink fire truck. Worse yet, we couldn't even get our local fire department to wear pink tee shirts for one day. Los Cruces, New Mexico had already made a success out of it, but Los Cruces wasn't Phoenix or Glendale. It wasn't Chicago. And it wasn't New York. It was clear that neither Phoenix nor Glendale was going to adopt the *Cares Enough to Wear Pink* program without something to motivate them.

I was livid. The fire chief was about my age, and had joined the fire department a short time before I had. We had known each other for about fifteen years and he was just a regular guy who had become fire chief, so I expected him to call me man to man, but that wasn't the case. In the meantime, I was having a $300,000 stainless steel statue being built, and was actively searching for my first fire truck. I had almost a full year to bring everything together and to begin to make a real difference in the lives of thousands of women. Unfortunately, I had just sold my home and had sunk what little money I had left over into the program. It was at that point I decided to seek help elsewhere.

The Pink Heals Concept

About a month after I was shot down by the Glendale Fire Department and was busy developing the first *Pink Ribbon Tour*, I ran into the brother of Tom Anson, a friend whom I hadn't seen in almost 20 years. Tom was a marketing genius. In his youth he tried acting, but ended up owning his own advertising and marketing agency in Chicago called MDI. So I called Tom, and we started hashing out a concept and tossing around ideas for a logo. Then he gets into my head, "Why are you doing this?" he asked. "Does someone in your family have cancer? Nobody just does something like this for the hell of it."

"I want to make an impact on women," I snapped, a little miffed at how someone could not understand the selflessness of what I wanted to do. "I want to help them and to go after cancer." Tom kept grilling me, "Why fire trucks and why pink?" It was frustrating the hell out of me. "It's like baseball," I explained. "When I pitched in a full stadium, and when every person was looking at me, I always threw a little harder and a little better than when I pitched in an empty stadium. The larger the crowd, the harder I would throw. In the bullpen I would throw 90 miles per hour, but on the pitcher's mound with the game on the line I'd throw 93. And the game is on the line for women with cancer. I want to make women and their families feel better when they're battling cancer. I want to inspire them. For women fighting cancer, each day is like going to the stadium and expecting no one to be there. I want them to feel like the stadium is packed with people that love them. So if everyone in the world wore pink for one day and we walked outside and just told a woman that we loved her, she would feel a little better. Feeling better is what it's all about. It's not about having a million dollars or giving her a cure she can't have, it's about making her feel loved."

"Then pink would heal?" Tom asked. "That's what I mean!" I exclaimed. I could almost hear Tom thinking. He paused, "Pink Heals it is. I'll put my staff on it and get back to you."

A couple days later Tom calls. He already had his staff working on details and developing a website and promotional material. I immediately registered and protected the name, because if I didn't, someone would surely snatch it up. It was unfathomable that with all the emphasis on pink, and with all the money being made from it, no one had already thought of it. It fit perfectly with my mission statement and conveyed the persona I wanted. Athlete. Firefighter. Machismo. And Caring. It's Pink Heals. The premise being that women are the color pink, and if the world was pink, every woman would feel better. Pink would heal everything. It would heal government. It would heal society. It would heal us. If we just acknowledged that women are the most important people in our lives and that if we took care of them, everything would be better.

Pink Turnout

The firefighters of the Guardians of the Ribbon were the first in the country to wear pink turnouts. Standard issue turnouts, often called "bunker gear," are the protective suits that firefighters wear to fight fires, but they are not pink. Ours had to be special made by Globe Manufacturing of Pittsfield, New Hampshire, which Wally Monsivaiz recommended. I called and explained what I was doing, and they graciously shut down their plant over a weekend and had the women in the garment area make six suits from material that they purchased. They even threw in an additional seven suits for free. Functional fire suits cost over $2000 because they are chemically treated, but the pink suits we use are not functional and cost approximately $700 each. For the *Pink Ribbon Tour*, the suits were a light pink, but for subsequent tours they were a rich fuchsia pink. Since the first tour, Globe is now in the pink turnout business and supplies them to fire departments all over the country. I tell every fire department I speak with that believes in what I am saying, that it needs to have one pink fire truck and at least one set of pink turnouts on hand, so one of their firefighters can attend charitable functions and represent women.

Pink turnout and tank.

Another consideration we faced was creating a corporate logo for *Guardians of the Ribbon* that would be immediately recognizable. We chose a pink version of the Maltese cross of awareness, love, hope, and rescue with a badge in the middle. We also have a

Guardian logo bearing the likeness of police and firefighters. *Cares Enough to Wear Pink* has always been our tagline and is associated with any logo worn on our backs. Why pink on everything? Because it heals.

Our logo.

Susan G. Komen for the Cure

During the early stages of developing the Cares Enough to Wear Pink program, I sought the endorsement of a large charitable organization, so I met with the *Susan G. Komen for the Cure* affiliate in Phoenix. I told them that I wanted to drive a pink fire truck across America to enlist firefighters to help raise money and to give it all to them. *Susan G. Komen* had raised millions for cancer research and had a profound impact in raising awareness in the fight against breast cancer. It had become the most recognizable cancer organization in the country and was synonymous with the color pink. I wanted in.

Being associated with *Susan G. Komen* seemed like the right thing at the time. Although I was pulling my Ribbon of Hope statue all over town with my pickup, I still did not have a fire truck, so I designed a concept fire truck with the *Susan G. Komen* name on it, and gave them the whole nine yards in hopes that they might come through with a real one. They did not, but they loved the concept because they would not have to spend any marketing dollars if I was out there doing the legwork for them. They also wanted to own my pink fire truck idea, but I decided to keep that for myself. While I was trying to buy a fire truck, I began towing my Ribbon of Hope statue to the homes of women who had cancer, and to other events, as a show of support, but apparently some of the women I supported weren't part of the *Susan G. Komen* network, and this ruffled some feathers. They began calling and warning me that if I wanted to be part of *Susan G. Komen* and for it to support me, I could not take my statue or a truck to a non-*Komen* event. *How can you get mad at me if I'm helping women with breast cancer?* I thought. *Aren't we working toward the same goal?*

At this point, I began wondering what I had gotten myself into. I had failed to see that any large corporation, no matter its intentions, is fraught with politics and ultimately becomes a bloated monster that consumes everything it can just because it can. Although *Susan G. Komen* was helping a lot of people, in my view, it wasn't helping some of the people who needed it most. Should I stay with them or go out on my own? Do I need its support or do I even want it? I was conflicted. But fortunately, a chance phone call from Rick Redmond, a friend in the marketing department of Louisville Slugger, one of the major suppliers of baseball bats for Major League Baseball, changed all that.

I had met Rick during the *Golf Across The USA Tour*, and he had given me a set of Louisville Slugger golf clubs. I told him about my new brainchild, what I wanted to do, and how I was going to help the world, and he offered to arrange a meeting with one of the marketing departments for Major League Baseball in California, which I readily accepted. In those early days, I would meet with anyone who might help because I knew the program was going to be a hit. I wanted to hear both positive and negative comments, so I could build upon strengths and address weaknesses. Everything I learned went into creating a better organization. So, I flew to Hollywood for lunch with the marketing people and explained that I wanted to drive pink fire trucks across America to honor women, and that I wanted to build symbolic pink fire stations of love and hope in communities throughout the country. The stations would not be pink color, but every brick and all building materials would bear the name of a woman or a family member who battled cancer. I also told them that I envisioned creating a Pink Heals clothing line from which profits would go to help families and to support efforts at the community level.

The executives were impressed with the Pink Heals concept, and from the widespread exposure of pink ribbons through the partnership of *Susan G.*

Komen and MLB, they recognized the potential for my program and offered encouragement and general support. However, I left that meeting knowing that I would never sell out my concept to a large national charity or to a corporate sponsor. If so, I feared that I would lose control over the mission statement, and that my program would be swallowed up and not reach the people who needed it. I had sold out to corporate sponsors during my golf tour and I still had a bad taste in my mouth. Everything from this point would stay in-house, and I would maintain control by doing a yearly tour where I could personally take my program into communities to ensure that 100 percent of the money raised by the program stayed in each local community. It was a major turning point in the program and a blessing to all the women and families battling cancer, so when I returned home, I jumped the *Susan G. Komen* ship and built my own ship, and I haven't looked back.

A Truck Named "Karen"

Three months before the inaugural 34-city *Pink Ribbon Tour* was to begin, I was under the gun. For almost a year, I had told anyone who would listen about how I was going to drive across America in a pink fire truck inspiring firefighters and everyone else to help raise money to battle the terrorist called cancer. I had great ideas, a solid plan, and I was ready to go to war. But I didn't have a way to get there.

For weeks, Lisa and I had been crisscrossing the Phoenix area pulling a two-ton ribbon with my pickup truck trying to raise enough money to buy a fire truck. Lisa was getting nervous, but in my mind, if I had to go to a junkyard and buy one, paint it with pink paint from Home Depot, and then tow it behind my pickup across the country, I was going to do it. I even asked the Phoenix Fire Department if they would lend me a truck, and although they said that they would love to help me out, they felt that with the economy being so bad, they didn't have a truck they could spare. Then I went to the Hall of Flame Fire Museum in Phoenix, which had about 90 fire trucks, and I asked if I could borrow one of theirs, but they were all antiques and they feared that none of them could make a trip across America without breaking down. Being an active, full-time firefighter in a large metropolitan area, and having made connections with fire departments across the nation, I reasoned that I should be able to locate a truck, but no such luck. But when all else fails, try Ebay.

Billy Futch claimed that his red, 1989 FMC, 28-foot, 12-ton, open cab, fire truck pumper ran like a sports car. And it did. At $13,000 it was not the cheapest truck on the market, but I had to have it. I trusted Billy. He was a firefighter in Jacksonville, Florida, and the owner of hireafiretruck.com, which rented fire trucks for special events. Even more telling was that he trusted me and held the truck until I could pay for it. I explained why I needed the truck and he bought into it without question. I assured him that I was going to have the money soon, although at the time I had no idea where it would come from.

A Starbucks Coffee shop was the last place I expected to find the money for a pink fire truck. One morning I joined several friends for coffee at my favorite Starbucks and, as usual, I began telling them about Guardians of the Ribbon, the *Cares Enough to*

Wear Pink program, and about my dream to launch a nationwide tour. It was then that I met Karen Hechler. She had just married a friend of mine and wanted to hear my ideas, so a few days later her husband, Dave, called saying that he and Karen wanted to meet me at Starbucks for coffee. She was waiting for me when I arrived and promptly wrote me a check for $13,000, the full cost of a fire truck. "Go for it, kid," she said. "Go buy that fire truck and do great things."

I was moved by Karen's generosity and immediately contacted Billy to tell him the great news. Sight unseen, my friend Steve Bogle and I, flew to Florida and sealed the deal with Billy in 30 minutes. We stayed the night and drove the diesel powered fire truck home the next day. But we almost didn't make it. On the way back, I mistakenly put several ounces of regular gasoline in the truck, and although the engine backfired and scared the hell out of us, we made it home on June 1, 2008.

With the *Pink Ribbon Tour* scheduled to begin on August 24, I had less than three months to turn a standard red fire truck into a pink symbol of hope. Maricopa Metals took the lead and put me in touch with a marketing company that wrapped trucks. Wrapping is a process of covering or shrink wrapping a vehicle with a colored vinyl skin containing any special artwork or designs. In this case, the truck was wrapped with a base pink color bearing small pink ribbons. But this turned out to be a mistake, because everywhere we went people associated the pink ribbons with breast cancer, which created the misperception that women with bone cancer, brain cancer, or other cancers, were not represented. On subsequent tours, the ribbons were removed, and the trucks were painted pink with our own Pink Heals – *Cares Enough to Wear Pink* brand of paint, so that we were not driving for just breast cancer or for a specific charity, but driving for all women.

About six months after the *Pink Ribbon Tour*, Karen was diagnosed with lung cancer, so we began naming our trucks after women who have had a profound impact on our organization and who had battled any cancer. Karen was the perfect choice. Without her selfless gift, the organization would not be where it is today, helping thousands of women in the fight against a deadly disease. Now that the *Cares Enough to Wear Pink* program is successful and growing into a worldwide movement, fire trucks are not as difficult to obtain, and people donate them frequently. At this

Karen signing "Karen".

writing, over 40 pink fire trucks represent the *Cares Enough to Wear Pink/Pink Heals Program* across the nation and in five foreign countries. But regardless of how many pink fire trucks grace the highways of this nation and others, "Karen" will always be the first.

Pink Heals Clothing

In the summer of 2008, I was driving around with my newly-acquired pink fire truck working out the bugs, while Lisa was getting everything else ready to go. Pamphlets were being printed, details were being hammered out, and cities were being selected for the inaugural *Pink Ribbon Tour*. So far, everything was a go, but our greatest concern was money. Since we neither had nor wanted corporate sponsors, we had to fund the tour ourselves, and the only way we could do it was to have people help us along the way and by selling *Cares Enough to Wear* Pink tee shirts.

Dave and Lisa in NYC.

Lisa has an incredible sense of fashion style and is the driving force behind our in-house clothing line for women. She also made one of the most important decisions in the formation of the Guardians of the Ribbon by not allowing me to give all the money away generated from our tee shirt sales to an organization in Phoenix that offered to give me $1 per shirt. A deal that would have allowed them to keep $10 per shirt

117

off all the labor and off all the love that the *Cares Enough to Wear Pink program* would create. Lisa took it upon herself to keep the sale of the clothing line in-house and to eliminate the middleman altogether, which increased our ability to keep our trucks fueled. Her decision to selflessly run the retail operation accomplished in three years what would have taken ten.

Proceeds from the sale of clothing are the lifeblood of our organization and we cannot survive without them. We ask people who think we are doing a job well done, and who appreciate what we are doing, to buy a tee shirt or something from our clothing line because it keeps our trucks on the road.

Meet and Greet

Not being one to like starting at the bottom of anything, I went straight to top of the firefighter food chain to build steam for the *Pink Ribbon Tour*. My first stop was the International Association of Fire Chiefs (IAFC) Conference in Denver, Colorado. I didn't ask or tell my fire chief because he wouldn't want me to go being an ordinary firefighter, so I drove my pickup truck some 900 miles to Denver loaded with folding tables and shirts and met the organizer, Shannon Gilliland, who gave me a space for free since I was a non-profit organization. Some local women even supplied some female volunteers to help sell tee shirts. After I arrived, I set up my display and put on my pink turnouts. As luck would have it, I was placed next to a booth of women firefighters who were promoting women in the fire service, and I began getting catcalls right away, "What next, pink skirts on the job?" the guys would yell. "Hey baby, where's the fire?" Some men would have been offended, but my personality was perfect for that. The chiefs would stand in front of my banner looking around, and there I was, a 6'2, 235-pound guy wearing pink turnouts pounding a pink Louisville Slugger bat into my hand. I would yell, "What am I, the pink elephant at the zoo? Some of the greatest things in life are right in front of your face. Until you ask a question you don't know what something is about?" Then I would act like I was chasing them down the hallway. It was great fun, but when I wasn't doing that, I was canvassing the conference area and visiting all the vendors and display tables. As the chiefs walked around collecting fliers, I handed out my brochures and talked to them about my upcoming tour. From that conference, I started a database and developed a relationship with fifteen or twenty fire chiefs in different parts of the country that wanted our tour to come through their area. Of course, my fire chief saw me, but he never came to the table, which I knew he wouldn't. But he was the reason I came in the first place. The conference provided some initial exposure and kicked me off nationally in a tax-based structure way. In fact, it was such a blessing and proved so valuable, that after the initial tour I decided to kick off each new tour from whichever city was hosting the conference.

Truck Signing

Two months earlier, on June 19, 2008, I was driving my pink fire truck in Phoenix when a total stranger pulled alongside yelling and motioning for me to pull over. Her name was Tracy Soto, and she asked if she could sign my truck. Little did she know that her act of love for a family member would be one of the most significant things to happen in the evolution of the *Cares Enough to Wear Pink* program. Beginning that day, it became my goal to have every person who suffers from cancer, or to have every person who has ever lost anyone to it, sign the truck as a tribute to their loved one, and as commitment toward helping to find a cure. A month later, Arizona Governor Janet Napolitano, now the Secretary of Homeland Security, signed the truck in front of the Arizona Capitol further validating the program.

Then Governor Janet Napolitano signs a truck.
She is currently Director of Homeland Security.

Those two signatures paved the way and helped personalize the struggle against a horrible disease. One month later, I launched the inaugural *Pink Ribbon Tour* and would collect over 50,000 additional names on every square inch of my pink fire truck. It was then that I realized the prevalence of the disease and how much pain it causes. I had to do something. The ball was in my hand.

CHAPTER 4
THE PINK RIBBON TOUR
BIRTH OF A MOVEMENT

Knowing that I was leaving Arizona for a two-month, 34-city *Pink Ribbon Tour/Cares Enough to Wear Pink Campaign*, I wanted to go out with a bang. I wanted hundreds of people to send us off in a spectacular display, and realizing that hundreds of roaring motorcycles make the greatest impact, I reached out to several motorcycle clubs in the area, and they were happy to escort us out of town. Now all I needed was an open place in a nice area where we all could all rally for a memorable sendoff. The Arrowhead Mall in Glendale was such a place.

Surprisingly, I got a phone call from my fire chief a few days before the tour. He realized that I was going ahead with it whether he liked it or not, and probably even more frustrating to him, was that he couldn't control it or prevent it. But just as I had done when I made a comeback in professional baseball in 1995, and during the Golf Across The USA Tour in 2003, I ensured that my job was safe by using my own vacation time and arranging that my shifts at work were covered. The last thing I needed was to be laid off while the fire department was still hiring! The fire chief wanted it to appear that he, the Glendale Fire

Department, and the firefighters union, supported me and the *Pink Ribbon Tour*, so they called me into a meeting with some people from the city marketing department, along with their many sycophants, who immediately surrounded me and began explaining how they could help. Whenever someone holds a meeting for my benefit, and I don't ask for it, alarms go off in my head. I didn't trust them, but I was cautiously excited that they wanted to help.

"We're going to help make this an enormous event," they said. "Let us know what we can do."

"Thank you," I said sincerely. "But Lisa and I have already contacted someone at the Arrowhead Mall. The *Pink Ribbon Tour* will kick off from there."

"Great!" They said. "Meet with Arrowhead and get all the permits. Let us know what you need, and what is going on, and don't worry about media coverage. We'll handle everything."

Now I was beginning to worry. Not only was I concerned about the fire chief and the city, but on Sunday, August 24, the morning that the tour was to begin, the pink fire truck's electrical system began acting up. Fortunately, Don Jessee swooped in and fixed it. I was still stressed out and worried whether all the bikers and other people would show, but when I arrived, the Air Force and fire trucks from the Peoria, Glendale, and other area fire departments, were already there, as were some 300 motorcycle riders raring to go. It was a huge event and visually spectacular, but my worst fear was soon realized. No media. Local coverage was not hard to get for an event of this size and significance, especially in my own hometown where I had contacts, but the media were clearly absent. In my mind, the fire chief set it up to look like they were going to help me, but they were really trying to spoil the kickoff and squash the tour. But it didn't work. A couple friends who believed in the fire department, called Channel 3, and they rushed out and filmed us as we were heading out of town toward Tucson escorted by a long chain of bikers dressed in pink. What a sight!

Once on the road, our first stop was in front of the Target store in Casa Grande, where we met several breast cancer survivors. From there, we went to Kohl's in North Tucson and met with four fire districts, including the Northwest Fire District, Tucson Fire, Rural Fire Department, and the Golden Ranch Fire District. The districts were all joining efforts and were committed to wearing pink on October 25-27, the three days that we designated as National Cares Enough to Wear Pink day. The movement had begun.

The Pink Ribbon Tour in the beautiful Arizona desert.

Life on the Road

Life on the road isn't easy. After the initial excitement and adrenaline wears off, it takes energy and commitment to live out of a suitcase and to put personal comfort on hold. As a professional baseball player in the minor leagues, I was used to long hours of travel by bus and staying in less than first class accommodations with little money. There's a huge difference between the major leagues and the minors, just ask anyone who has suffered through an endless cycle of long, boring bus rides, fast food joints, and occasional stays at a seedy No Tell Motel. But that's the price one has to pay for the dream of playing in the big leagues, a dream that most players, including myself, never realize. And then there was the Golf Across The USA Tour, where I spent seven grueling months on the road in a golf cart sleeping in my truck, at fire stations, and in hotels often paid for by generous individuals or from my own pocket. However, the Pink Ribbon Tour wasn't about baseball or golf. It was so much more.

The entire team consisted of Lisa at home, the three guys in the truck, and me. Wally Monsivaiz from the Las Cruces, New Mexico Fire Department, along with his brother-in-law, Chris Torres, and my friend, Steve Bogle, comprised the crew. No others helped us except for some friends I had met on the *Golf Across The USA Tour*, which was essentially the proving ground for the *Pink Ribbon Tour*. Rather than reinventing the wheel, I followed much the same route as I did on the golf tour, because I knew I had reliable contacts in some of the cities that I had visited before. The golf tour, although it was not a success in my eyes, built an alliance and trust between me and a lot of the men and women across the country who saw me golf on behalf of kids. They knew that I was credible and they believed in what I was doing.

Having an established support base was a huge benefit and helped ease some of my pre-tour apprehension. Breaking down at the side of the road, or getting a flat tire in a golf cart, is a far cry from blowing a head gasket in the middle of nowhere in a 12-ton pink fire truck, and having friends and solid contacts most everywhere I went was comforting. But having little money was not.

With only about $1000 in our account and a credit card to buy gas and hotels, we just started driving across country with a bunch of tee shirts that Lisa had designed. We were like a traveling ministry. We went and set up at a location, and when people saw us, they wondered what we were doing, and stopped by and listened to what we had to say. We gave them the information, and if they bought into it, they purchased a tee shirt to help support the program, which helped us move to the next town. We developed the Cares Enough to Wear Pink tee shirts because we needed something on tour to generate money for our expenses. On the first tour, we only had two styles of shirts and we only brought about 500 shirts with us. If we were at a truck stop and doing well, our sales paid for our fuel. Our tank held 50 gallons of diesel fuel and we got 8 miles per gallon, which meant we could drive 400 miles on one tank. To make matters worse, fuel costs climbed to an all-time high that summer and neared $5 per gallon. This put a pinch in everyone's budget, but the money part took care of itself when people heard our message.

Wherever we went, we tried to convince people to donate hotel rooms or to get communities to give us some fuel. One time, we went and sat in front of a fire station, but no one showed up, so we had a place to sleep or sit for ten hours. We did not want any of the money from events that were hosted by local fire and police going to our organization for anything other than fuel or expense money. The events were to inspire thousands of fire and police agencies to get in pink for their women, and then to raise money for their own cancer organizations, not to make anyone rich or to support us.

Most times, we were invited by friends to make stops, but they often didn't know what to expect from us. We showed up and basically generated our own media. In the beginning, I only had a laptop computer and a cell phone, and I would target five or six points of interest and then send out a press release, pamphlet, or video, to each city manager, mayor, and fire and police chief. I would also send letters to women's auxiliaries and hospitals, letting them know that we were coming to town to explain a free program that could help them help their own community. But it was also a test to see what kind of community leadership they had, and to gauge their willingness to try something new to help benefit their citizens. People were invited to bring their entire families and to bring their own tents or motor homes to the events. Some stops were unbelievable, and others we just sat in a parking lot waiting for people to show. But regardless of where we went, we spread our message and stayed strong. However, we realized about half way through the tour that we had to get rid of the pink ribbons on the truck. At one of the events, a lady with bone cancer was dejected at the erroneous notion that she couldn't sign the fire truck because she didn't have breast cancer. When she saw the pink ribbons, she felt like she wasn't getting any love, and she just sat at a picnic table removed from everyone else until we explained to her that our pink truck represented all women, not just those with breast cancer. This was the turning point, and from then on, we began representing all women, and it remains that way today.

Pink Ribbon Tour 2008

The 2008 *Pink Ribbon Tour* would be a success— and everyone knew it. Or at least I did. On August 25, one day into the tour, people from all over the country began calling me asking if the pink fire truck could come to their town. When I was in Los Cruces, New Mexico, the Memphis [Tennessee] Fire Department wanted me to come to their city, but I had to say no with a promise to come on the next tour. And there were others too, but I only had so much time off before I had to get back to my job at the fire department. It was hard for me to refuse anyone. I would have stayed on the road for a year if I could have, but there were times when I also made unscheduled stops, like in South Bend, Indiana where the wife of a fire chief called and asked if we would stop on our way to Chicago. They even talked about painting a reserve truck to fundraise for the women of South Bend.

After spending a couple days in New Mexico, it was on to Ozona, Texas, one of the best small towns in the country. I stopped by in 2003 when I golfed across the country and developed some lasting friendships. The people at the fire department were surprised when I dropped by with my pink fire truck, and they went out of their way by providing me with a new spare tire and by rewiring the trailer and fixing some lights. If you happen to be driving to San Antonio going east or El Paso going west, stop at the firehouse and ask for Miss Lou. She runs the station and can rally all the fire personal for a meet and greet in short notice. And don't forget to eat at the Hitching Post restaurant and have a British Hamburger. To this day it is the best hamburger I have ever had.

Our next stop was Universal City just outside of San Antonio, where the people at the fire department housed the truck and our Ribbon of Hope statue. They were very excited about the stop and assured us that they would sport pink for our women during the three days in October, and that they would rally other cities to do the same. Then it was on to Austin, where we were put up in a very nice hotel. At that time, the city was planning on having the Lance Armstrong Foundation there, along with other cancer organizations. The festivities included guest speakers, snow cone machines, and even a performance by country and western superstar and breast cancer survivor, who at that time was dating Lance Armstrong. We were so proud of the truck and what it stood for, and to have had the city of Austin take notice of this truck and use it to inspire their city.

Dallas

We made two stops in the Dallas area at Station 2 in Irving, and at Station 1 in Grapevine. The chief of Irving came out to see the truck, along with all the men from Station 2, and he thanked us for our work as firefighters and gave us their honorary coin of excellence. He too, planned to have his department do something to honor the women of Irving. Then we visited the Grapevine Fire Department to say hello to the guys, and were impressed with the reception we got, especially since we were uninvited. We shared stories and had a few laughs over dinner, and then they took us to the Hilton where they got us two rooms for the night, courtesy of their union president, and discussed having us back next year and designing shirts of their own to honor their women.

Everybody loves a parade.

Houston

Houston was our biggest and best stop yet thanks to Deborah Schmidt from the Harris County Sheriff's office. She rallied the three agencies in Houston, along with their community leaders, to support the *Cares Enough to Wear Pink Campaign* and to put on a great show for the event. It was the kind of grass roots involvement that I had envisioned when I conceived the tour and was a shining example of what great things the common citizen can accomplish when they are inspired by a noble and just cause. The following are a few comments that were posted on our blog after our visit:

"Pink and Blue All Over said... Leather, vinyl, plastic, it really doesn't matter. What matters is that they are doing something positive (raising awareness) to help fight a terrible disease. It hasn't taken a dime from any research, treatment or other services as it is all privately funded. When they drove out of Houston this morning I saw HOPE driving out of town - and that is what must happen to bring hope to others. Go visit the truck if you are lucky enough to have it stop in your town..."

A lovely lady signs our truck in Texas.

"Inpink said... Dave and guys, I want to tell you how much I enjoyed the truck and your message when you were in Irving, Texas. As

a survivor, it makes it so awesome to see you guys getting the word out and also getting more men to participate. It sometimes takes smaller, hands on organizations and groups to get the word out and see how a difference you can make. Komen and ACS are great but it is nice to have support from people like you...you can also put a face to the support not just a website . . . Amy Pitman. Keller, Texas"

Me, Wes Malcolm, and Steve Countryman.

"L8ENPINK said... If passion drives you, let reason hold the reins. ~Benjamin Franklin. Thank you Dave and Guardians of the Ribbon. My family and I support YOU and give Thanks for what you are doing. Keep on truckin'...Thank you for having such a PASSION to get others to truly see PINK! Your dedication and determination will NEVER be forgotten. Thank you! Thank you! Thank you! Being a SURVIVOR, and seeing a PINK fire truck really takes my breath away... and reassures me that there still is hope in finding a CURE!"

The Jasper Effect

On the freeway about a mile outside of Jasper, Texas we began having problems with our trailer hitch, so we pulled over at a nearby truck shop to have it repaired. We were all hungry, and fortunately, a convenience store sat just across the highway. While the trailer was being fixed, we crossed the road and went over to get something to eat, but as we got

Jasper

closer, we heard yelping coming from a huge empty bait tub bearing a "Free Puppies" sign. We looked inside and there was only one Black Lab puppy about eight weeks old. Gavin Henderson, a local resident, had spotted three puppies on the side of the highway and brought them to work at the store. Two males had already been given away, leaving the last puppy all alone. We couldn't have that, so we got together and decided to adopt a fire dog, and to name him Jasper.

Jasper was an instant hit and grew up on our pink fire truck. It got to the point that when we arrived at a hotel for the night, he'd run right to the hotel room and sit and wait, and then when we got up in the morning, he'd run out and hop up on the fire truck. He slept on top of the cowling between the front driver and the captain where it was warm.

We got a lot of positive support and feedback from Jasper. He was a great icebreaker to rally more people into our program, and when the story got out that we had saved a dog that had been abandoned alongside a highway near Jasper, and that we brought him with us on a tour to help women with cancer, he became a huge celebrity. Women constantly fawned over him and ensured that he was healthy and happy. He would hang out at the events, and acted like he was a year old. He followed me everywhere I went and never strayed too far, but I was always a little worried that he'd run out onto the freeway and get hit. I kept thinking, *if this dog dies on tour I'll make national headlines, but not in a good way*, so I gave him to my daughter's boss. Today, he enjoys a life of luxury in a beautiful home, but he will always hold a special place in my heart and in the hearts of thousands of women across the country. It was meant to be.

Beaumont

The City of Beaumont, Texas, Chief Ann Huff, and Captain Brad Pennison, made us feel very welcome. They were the first city to escort us with lights and sirens on the freeway and through town. They made us lunch, arranged a press conference, and gave us two nights lodging for free. I had asked that each city we visited give us something to add to the truck, so that when I got home it would reflect the love that we received from across the country. Beaumont Fire gave us a horn, a monitor, and another light bar. What a great show of support!

From Beaumont we had planned to visit Jacksonville, Florida, but we got a last minute message not to come because of the terrible string of storms that were to hit that part of the country. Instead, we diverted north to Vicksburg, Mississippi picking up followers along the way. Everywhere we went we built support and enlisted the backing of firefighters, police, city leaders, and the citizens of each community. In two short weeks, we felt that we had made a difference and increased awareness of cancer and its horrible effects.

We left Beaumont and headed north to Shreveport, Louisiana, and then made our way east toward Birmingham, Alabama, when around 7 p.m., we noticed that the truck alternator wasn't charging. We stopped near a Pilot Truck Stop in Raeville to check it out, and our hunch was right. But as luck would have it, a USA Truck Repair shop was right there. Jeff, the owner, offered to install a new alternator at cost and to donate the four hours of labor. Jeff's selfless act was yet another example of the outpouring of love and generosity we encountered on the tour.

Four Hours later, we were on the road again and headed for Birmingham. We only got two hours into the drive and couldn't go any longer, so we stopped in Clinton, Mississippi for the night. When we got up the next morning, a women's organization that was staying at the same hotel came by the truck and shared some stories with us, and bought some shirts. Of course, several of them were cancer survivors and gladly signed the truck. Then the Clinton High School cheerleaders came by for a photo opportunity with the truck. Word travels fast!

South Carolina

Ten miles outside of Savannah, Georgia, twelve motorcycles were waiting to escort us into Walterboro, South Carolina. Alan Duke, President of the Red Knights Motorcycle Club, along with Gary, TM's, Mike from Full Throttle Magazine, and many others, took care of us for the two days while we were there, and it was exactly how I imagined it would be. We visited hospitals, malls, schools, restaurants, and many other locations in Charleston and in the surrounding towns. The fire chiefs from Walterboro, Summerville, Ashley River, North Charleston, Old Fort, Charleston, and others helped us create so much awareness that all we had to do was drive up, park, put on our pink gear, and just sit back and let all the wonderful ladies sign the truck and share their stories with us. It wasn't long before we were running out of room on the truck. We had thousands of signatures on the truck, and even Jasper, our faithful puppy, was dressed in pink. We didn't need to do anything anymore. The truck was now telling a great story all by itself, and the importance of celebrating the truck and the *Cares Enough to Wear Pink Campaign* was growing with every stop. The beauty of the truck was that it not only supported all the healthy women and the cancer survivors, but it also carried the names of so many women who had passed due to cancer. It was truly a rolling memorial, a symbol of hope, and a rallying point. As we drove across the country, we witnessed fire departments starting their own *Cares Enough to Wear Pink Campaigns* to help raise money for the women of their communities. We only wanted to help generate the passion behind the idea by driving this truck and meeting all these great people. The work was theirs and we were honored to be part of it.

A little girl and her hero.

Our next destination was Myrtle Beach, South Carolina. Bill and Renee Collins picked us up about fifty miles outside of town and escorted us to the Dead Dog Saloon restaurant, where we attended a fundraiser for firefighters in the area in honor of 9-11. We met some great folks and then went to the Imaging Center, where we were greeted by a bunch of screaming ladies who serenaded us. James, a firefighter from nearby Midway Fire, invited us to his home the following morning to wash the truck and to have coffee. While we were there, we decided to visit his daughter's middle school to show the truck and to talk to the kids, which we all love to do. Thanks to Bill and Renee, who got us hotel rooms right on the beach, we went to sleep that night listening to the ocean. It was a great experience.

Our brothers in blue escorting us.

The next morning it was on to Raleigh-Durham, North Carolina, and to another extraordinary event. With less than three weeks warning, two great cities came together and rallied around our truck like no other. There were so many fire trucks, firefighters, and EMS personnel in one place that it was difficult to move around. Maria from Durham Fire, and Kristy from Raleigh Fire, put on a great show of support for the pink fire truck. Both cities actively promote their own awareness and fundraising programs for their own charities and did a wonderful job in every aspect. It was great to see so many visionary leaders willing to add to the list of charities that we in the public safety already support, and to see civic action at work. The Raleigh-Durham area is progressive and vibrant, and was a pleasure to visit. What a job they did on short notice!

"PinkPassion BC Survivor said... Raleigh and Durham you ROCK! Your support to every survivor and to the continued need of awareness is FABULOUS! I have key chain I carry which states, "3 million women in the United States are living with breast cancer. Only 2 million know about it." Awareness is mandatory to save each and every precious life. We women cannot do it all alone we need the support of our men. Again, Raleigh Durham...YOU ROCK! And a shout out to Dave and the Crew...YOU ROCK!"

The crew from Virginia Beach.

We concluded our tour of the central eastern seaboard with a stop at the mall in Virginia Beach, where the mayor and over 100 firefighters clad in pink greeted us. The mayor issued a proclamation making October 15th the *Cares Enough to Wear Pink Day* by the Citizens of Virginia Beach, and the 25th, 26th and 27th of October the days that public safety wears pink. The mayor reminded me a lot of my hometown mayor, Elaine Scruggs, in that they are both visionary and forward thinking, which left us wondering how much the organization would grow between now and the next time we visited.

DC to NYC

Initially, I was scared to take pink fire trucks to the East Coast because the men there have the reputation of being tough, hardworking guys; steel workers, longshoremen, construction workers. I feared that they weren't going to embrace pink like the rest of the country, but when I got there and met the men and their families, and when they found out that this was a job well done, they embraced me and took the program to the next level.

The people in Washington DC and Station 6 were great to us. The fire chief and several of the assistant chiefs came out to meet us and arranged for the media to come to the station and help publicize our project. Battalion Chief Mike Donlon then invited us to visit the National Fire Academy, and for the next two days, he toured us around the area and provided contacts for our upcoming stop in the Philadelphia area. Mike and the rest of the gang at the National Fire Academy provided a signal service to the *Pink Ribbon Tour* and will be on our national tour every year. We also made a surprise visit to retired National Fire Chief Charlie Dickinson's home to give his wife a gift and let her sign the fire truck. Below is a touching letter that I received from Charlie Dickinson shortly after our visit:

"After 44 years associated with the fire service, I retired this past April of 08 from the United States Fire Administration, and my wife Lily and I were excited about all the things we had planned to do, and now would have the time to do so. Life has a funny way though, more often than not, in setting what your priorities will actually be. So it was for us. Lily was diagnosed with Breast Cancer in August of 08 as a result of her annual mammogram. Within a month, extensive surgery and treatment began as Lily began that journey that literally thousands upon thousands of women have traveled before her. She, Lily, had lost her mother and two of four sisters to breast cancer, with another sister having had a mastectomy as a result of breast cancer...

Lily had her surgery (Double Mastectomy) including beginning reconstruction, and was at home resting and recovering on the evening of September the 20th when I received a phone call from District of Columbia Battalion Chief Mike Donlon, who wanted to ensure that Lily was home, for there was "Something" on the way to our home she needed to see. We had no idea what he was referring to, and wasn't sure about visitors with Lily's current condition. But it mattered not for something was on the way.

Shortly, there was the wail of a siren and red lights flashing with of all things, a "Pink Pumper" towing a trailer with a huge "Breast Cancer Ribbon" that left no doubt this fire pumper and its attending crew was spreading awareness of breast cancer and its risk and effects on women with the "Cares Enough to Wear Pink" Campaign!

In they came, Captain Dave Graybill and his crew along with National Fallen Firefighter Foundation staff members Bev Walters, Judy Whitlow, and Becky Nusbaum, as well as BC Mike Donlon. Ensuring that Lily was okay, they ever so gently escorted her outside with the rest of us following and showing her the pumper, while Dave explained their journey through all the cities they had been to, as well as ones they would be going to in the following weeks. Let it suffice to say Lily was, in fact all us were not just impressed, but amazed that Dave had organized this "Pink Pumper" and was touring the country to bring awareness to this dreaded disease being breast cancer!

Lily added her signature to the hundreds already signed on the pumper, and after a few pictures, not to mention amazed neighbors and friends, off they went. Captain Graybill and crew headed for Philadelphia the next day continuing their tour.

After everyone was gone, and with quiet reflection, Lily said, "While it's heartbreaking to see all those names on the pumper, it's heartwarming knowing that so many, thru the "Pink Pumper's" tour, are united and supportive

141

of one another, and most importantly, bringing awareness to thousands of others to continue to press for more funds for research, treatment and hopefully someday, a cure for breast cancer.

No other words are needed, other than thanks Dave, to you and your crew, for a terrific job and success of your "Cares Enough to Wear Pink" Campaign!" --Charlie Dickinson

More Big Apple

Although everyone had been extremely kind and supportive of the *Pink Ribbon Tour* up to this point, it was especially important for me to go back to New York City because I didn't get any fire department support there during the golf tour. Prior to entering New York City, Lisa and some family of the drivers had joined us in New Jersey for a tour of East Rutherford. The city assigned a police officer to stand guard with the truck overnight since it had become quite valuable with all the signatures on it. The next morning we had a parade through town, but during the parade, the trailer hitch snapped right in the middle of the road. Within minutes, the police chief and the fire department called in a city welder who worked on it nonstop for four hours so we could get to NYC. Meanwhile, we resumed the parade with just the fire truck. A very special thanks goes out to Carlstadt Police and Fire departments, and to the Woodbridge Police Department for helping us out.

Since we were behind schedule, I called the police department in New York City saying that we were arriving in a pink fire truck and to be expecting us. An East Rutherford police officer escorted us toward the Lincoln Tunnel where another policeman was waiting.

"Do you have a permit?" he asked.

"I don't' need a permit," I said. "Just take me to the Lincoln Tunnel."

The East Rutherford police then led us to the entrance where the Port Authority was waiting. They put their hands down on the desk, "Who are you guys?"

I then went through my whole spiel. "Are you going to fit through the tunnel?" they asked.

Everyone just looked at one another. We had cleared dozens of underpasses on our drive east, but of course, I didn't measure the ribbon statue everywhere I went. The Lincoln Tunnel is exactly 13 feet in height, but I was unsure of the height of our Ribbon of Hope statue, and if it would fit through the tunnel. The pressure was beginning to mount. The New York City Police were on the inside waiting for us, and I was blocking traffic. I always said that if we got stuck it would be good for publicity, so away we went. We cleared it by about four inches. Lisa looked over at me and sighed, "We did it."

When we got to the other side of the tunnel a New York City motorcycle cop was waiting. "Where are we supposed to go?" he asked.

"I don't know," I said. "I thought you guys had something planned."

The cop shrugged. "I was just told to be here."

"Take me to Rockefeller Center!" I demanded, having neither the permission nor the necessary permits. I had seen Rockefeller Center on TV many times, and I had always wanted to go there, so off we went. We turned left then we turned right, and the cop says, "I'm outta here! Just keep going and you'll run right into it."

So now we're driving our pink fire truck unescorted through New York City traffic, and we get to an open side of Rockefeller Center where the bands play. Giant rubber pylons block the street and I put my lights on. A security guard comes up, "What are you doing?"

"I'm supposed to be in here right now," I bluffed.

"No one told me."

I then told him to move the pylons so I could get out of traffic, and he does, and we pull up alongside Rockefeller Center and put our turnouts on and begin passing out fliers. Suddenly, three big guys in suits with earphones looking like Special Forces operators come over and challenge me. "What are you doing?"

"You didn't know?"

"No!" they barked. "Know what?"

"Well, I'm supposed to be here."

"Well, you don't have a permit. We don't know anything about it. We can't allow you to be here."

"The women that have signed the trucks said we can be here."

The men looked hard at me. "Hold on a minute."

The men went inside, and a half hour later, they returned and said that we would have to leave because of insurance liability. But they did tell us how to get to Radio City Music Hall, where we illegally parked for four hours until dark. I love New York City!

We concluded our stay in the Big Apple with a stop in Central Valley to pay a special visit to Katina Chontos, one of our biggest supporters who had been instrumental in helping us for about seven months. She set us up with a place to stay, and all our meals where taken care of by the Bright Star Diner. Her friends from the diner even made sure that we had coats to wear so our tender Arizona bodies would not get cold. While we were there we had a static display of the truck right on the road in front of the diner. People that drove by all waved and honked, and made us feel welcome.

Kicking up our heels at Radio City Music Hall.

New Hampshire

One day short of a month into the tour, we left New York and visited Globe Manufacturing, the company that made our pink turnouts. Lisa Wickman and Stephanie McQuade from Globe, along with the support of all 350 employees, did a wonderful job putting on events in Concord and Pittsfield during our stay. They even got a local band and representatives from the American Cancer Society to come out and support us.

> *"rbfarley said... It was a great honor to escort the Pink Ribbon Tour into New Hampshire and to be part of the festivities in Concord. This is a great group of people doing wonderful work for a great cause. Godspeed to you all. Rob*

Farley, Deputy State Fire Marshal NH State Fire Marshal's Office; Captain Pembroke, NH Fire Department."

After the festivities in New Hampshire, we drove nine hours through the night to make it to Reading, Pennsylvania for a meeting with the mayor. Of course, the firefighters gave us an escort, and even took our truck to their shop to fix a leak in our radiator. After the meeting and a good night's sleep, we were off to Lancaster for a great reception, followed by a trip to Harrisburg, where we took part in a meet and greet with local politicians, including Pennsylvania State Senator Lisa Baker, who offered the following:

"I baker said... Dave - On behalf of the entire Pennsylvania Senate, please accept our thanks for the good work of the Pink Ribbon Tour honoring and supporting families and women touched by breast cancer. We appreciated your stop in Harrisburg on September 24th. And we wish you continued safe travels during the remainder of your 2008 tour. - Senator Lisa Baker."

State Senator Lisa Baker (center) welcomes the Guardians of the Ribbon.

We wrapped up the Pennsylvania leg in Pittsburgh, where Fire Chief Francis DeLeonibus stayed with us for two days to make sure the fire truck was safe and that we had everything we needed. I also touched base with an old friend, Jim Flaherty, vice-president of Local Union #1. Jim supported me when I came through on a golf cart during my 2003 tour. On our way out of town we paid a special visit to his daughter Jamie, who is a cancer survivor, at her work and snapped some great pictures of her signing the truck.

Our next stop was at University Heights Station 1 outside Cleveland, where the fire department had already made hundreds of Cares Enough to Wear Pink tee shirts to help raise money for two specific charities in their own community. It was inspiring to see people embracing our concept and developing a systemic approach to implementing it. Even more inspiring were the people we met at the rally. One young lady, Susan Dambro, was so moved by the pink fire truck that the next day we traveled 70 miles to Ashland, Ohio to visit her mother who was a survivor of breast cancer. After Susan had her mom sign the truck, we sat her in the captain's seat, and put all her kids in the back and took them on a ride through town. We then took the truck to her 13-year-old daughter's soccer game to cheer her on, and while we were there, all the ladies in the crowd who had fought cancer came over and signed the truck. Susan was truly an inspiration and helped to remind us why we were doing what we were doing.

We then traveled to Ohio for two stops. The first was in Dayton, where Hayley Fudge from Lion Apparel did a great job putting on an event at their corporate headquarters. We also received proclamations from

Mayor Rhine McLin and from the United States Senate by way of Senator Sherrod Brown. Then it was on to Toledo, where the fire department allowed us to do a static display of the fire truck from their fire station #25 for four hours, and then set us up with hotel rooms for the night. They also let us keep the truck at their local shop to keep it safe and even fueled the fire truck up for us before we left.

Clay County, Indiana shouts out.

Clay Fire Department outside of South Bend, Indiana was another department that set the bar high for the *Pink Ribbon Tour*. Their goal was to get all the fire departments in the state to wear pink work shirts for the women of their communities, and if their enthusiasm is any indication of success, it won't be long before everyone in the state will be wearing pink.

Not to be outdone, Schererville, Indiana went all out. They had requested for us to come and were ready and waiting when we arrived. Shirts were already being worn and there was even a pink ambulance parked in front of city hall to greet us. We talked a little about our program, and then there was a celebration for their women, and especially the breast cancer survivors. These cities are all starting to have their shirts done and already being distributed around the towns. Thanks go out to Schererville for having great vision for their women.

Fishers City, Indiana.

Countryside, Illinois Cares Enough.

The next day we fought through the Chicago traffic to the suburb of Countryside on the northwest side of the city. When we arrived at Westfield Mall, the fire department already had their trucks there with their ladder high in the air flying our banner. Equally as impressive was that all their firefighters were wearing pink work shirts. They saw that wearing pink uniform shirts not only showed support for the fight against cancer, but also for the women of their communities. Kudos to them and their vision.

On October 6, we rolled into Springfield, Illinois to a rousing reception. Several other organizations that support the fight against breast cancer were already there, so we joined in on the fun. The planners of the event made us feel right at home with food, a big screen TV with the Bears game on, and plenty of babysitters for Jasper. It was evident that a lot of planning went into the event in a short amount of time and that the city took its fight against cancer seriously.

Two days later, we traveled west to Missouri and visited Wentzville and a few surrounding towns. Dave Marlo, Chief Randy BornHop, and the gang from Wentzville Fire really took care of us. They let us stay in a new station that hadn't been opened yet and they escorted us everyday wherever we went. They planned events and even had our truck serviced free of charge, which was not cheap. Our Pink Fire Truck needed the bearings packed on the left front wheel, new shocks, and a front end alignment, and they even threw in a new front tire. Peggy and the great women from Ann's Bra Shop worked hand-in-hand with the firefighters so that all the events went smoothly. Our last event at Ann's Bra Shop was our most memorable and inspiring. Each one of us, over 150 in all, released a pink balloon into the air in celebration of the *Pink Ribbon Tour* and in acknowledgment of all the women whose signatures appeared on the truck.

Up, up, and away!

But something occurred after the event at Ann's Bra Shop that I'll never forget. While we were there we had heard about Ginger, a beautiful woman who was battling for her life against breast cancer, and we were asked by a friend and her family if we could come by and see her. Ginger had been battling her second occurrence for about 6 months, and the family thought if we came by in the pink fire truck dressed in our pink turnouts it would lift her spirits. As she made her way to the front door, she was shocked at the sight of us standing there. She was so weak and tired that it was hard for her to show any emotion, but when she saw Jasper she broke out into a smile and wanted to love on him. It was pure magic. Jasper had become an important part of the tour and it made a huge difference just having him with us. When all of us got in the truck for the drive back there was dead silence. Our visit with Ginger had driven home the importance of what we were doing like nothing else could.

A moving scene as Cammie Holiday rides the truck in Wentzville.

The next three days saw us make stops in Columbia, Missouri, at the Shawnee Mission Fire Department outside of Kansas City, and at Topeka, Kansas. Over 100 firefighters and community leaders in Topeka greeted us with a round of applause as we turned the corner and made us feel right at home. Teri Troth and her husband Mike, a fire captain for Topeka Fire, created a huge event for us and had the fire department wearing their new uniforms to honor the Cares Enough to Wear Pink Days. I had met Teri online and she had told me she was just diagnosed with cancer, and she had asked if I would visit her in the pink fire truck. It was impossible to say no to an angel.

Denver

Mid-October weather in the Rocky Mountains is unpredictable at best, and had it not been for an untimely snow and cold, Wendy Forbes of Broomfield would have surely put on the greatest event of the *Pink Ribbon Tour*. She rallied fourteen different fire and police departments to attend the event and also got them to commit to the Cares Enough to Wear Pink Days. More importantly, all departments committed to planning fundraisers to support women within their communities. In addition, Kathy Novak, the mayor of North Glenn, and Broomfield mayor Patrick Quinn, issued proclamations honoring our work and the Cares Enough to Wear Pink Days. A quick stop in Aurora, Colorado concluded our trip through the Centennial State.

Bountiful, Utah was our next stop and was everything its name implied. Located to the north of Salt Lake City, this picturesque town was the second settlement in the state and where I first learned of Lindsey, a young lady I will never forget.

We had just finished a program in Bountiful, and were driving through a small neighborhood when a woman stops us in traffic and runs up to the truck crying. "You're not leaving are you?"

I said that we had to go to the next city. She explained that she had driven over two hours to see us, and then asks if she can sign our truck. "Is it for you?' I asked.

"No, it's for my daughter."

I didn't believe her initially, because this woman was probably in her late twenties or early thirties. "Your daughter?"

"Yes, my daughter. She's 13 years old and is in the 7th grade. She just had a double mastectomy."

Reality hit me square in the face. For almost two months, I had been out on the road at war and had met all sorts of people with cancer. I had heard hundreds of horror stories, and I had become pretty emotionally resilient, but Lindsey's story struck deep. It hurts when

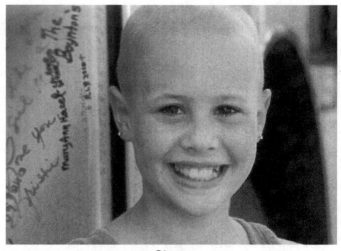

Chase

children get cancer or any disease for that matter. One of the most difficult aspects of the Cares Enough to Wear Pink program is going to a cancer ward in a children's hospital or hearing about a child battling for their life against a disease they cannot understand. Our mission is to help all people through our women, but it seems like we visited a lot of children's hospitals and saw more and more children afflicted with cancer. People say that cancer is on the rise because of our diet or that because we smoke, but five-years-olds getting cancer. I don't know what it is, but we've got to stop it.

North Las Vegas

North Las Vegas pulled out all the stops and made our stay the best so far. Nancy O'Connor, Cedrick Williams, and the chiefs from North Las Vegas were unbelievable and met our every need. They tuned up the truck, made us a new set of pink turnouts, and gave us a Pink SCBA (self-contained breathing apparatus) so that our outfits were complete. They even put us up in the Cannery Hotel, which tossed in coupons for free food. The hotel was outstanding in every way, and it even had a movie theatre where we could relax and get some down time. But the fun didn't stop there. During the fundraising event, we were given a Proclamation by the mayor of North Las Vegas, and we also received acknowledgement by then Governor of Nevada, Jim Gibbons. Senator Harry Reid also presented us with a Certificate of Commendation, and his office helped us get clearance with the Secret Service and FBI to attend an event in Henderson for then vice-presidential candidate Joe Biden. But more importantly, North Las Vegas sold almost a thousand shirts to the public to raise money for an organization in their community that helps women with cancer. And that's what the *Pink Ribbon Tour* was all about.

Los Angeles

After nearly two months on the road, we rolled into the City of Angels on a natural high. We had been invited to attend a taping of the Bonnie Hunt Show and to appear as guests along with famous singer and actress, Olivia Newton John, who was a friend of Bonnie's and a cancer survivor. Our greatest concern was sliding down a fire pole in pink turnouts on national TV, blowing out a knee, and then needing to call 9-1-1 on her show. Two of us weren't firefighters to begin

Olivia Newton John and me after taping.

with, and neither of us who were firefighters had poles at our fire stations nor had we ever slid down one. We were a little nervous, but everything worked out fine. The highlight of the day was Olivia signing the truck. She jumped right in and drove it down the lot like she worked for the Glendale Fire Department. She was a lot of fun and spent time with us before, during, and after the show. The next day, we wrapped up our visit to Los Angeles with a static display in front of City Hall with the L.A. Fire Department.

Hamming and Cheesing with the stars.

The final stops on the 2008 *Pink Heals Tour* were at the Sycuan Fire Department and the Sycuan Casino Resort outside of San Diego, where we were given a warm Southern California welcome. Everybody had pink on and there was not a dry eye in the area as we pulled into the Casino. It was there that I was interviewed for a story that would appear in a national magazine and drive a wedge between me and the leadership of the Glendale Fire Department. But after two long months on the road, my thoughts turned to home.

Lisa and some of the girls threw us a huge party at the Pink Bridge in old downtown Scottsdale when we arrived. We were led into town by the same motorcycle group that escorted us out two months earlier, and several booths and picnic tables were set up. Cammie Holiday and Monica Morales helped Lisa set up, and about 500 people attended. For three hours we celebrated the trucks and a job well done. Even the Scottsdale Fire Department was there because they had adopted the pink shirts along with the fire department from the Air Force Base. It was good to be home.

Aftermath

The inaugural *Pink Ribbon Tour* was an outstanding success. In less than one year I went from hearing about a fire department that was wearing pink shirts to support their women who battle cancer, to driving a pink fire truck pulling a $300,000 statue of a ribbon around the country, all on a whopping budget of $3,800 with no marketing company, no PR firm, and no sponsors. Many said it couldn't be done, but when the power of love and the passion to make a difference in a huge way are combined for a good cause and supported by dedicated people, anything can be accomplished. Each year, women of this country vote on the professions that they most admire and respect, and often firefighters are at the top of the list. Knowing this and realizing the high quality of leadership that most fire chiefs possess, it was a "no brainer" when it came to asking our public safety to spearhead the effort to "GO PINK" in honor of our women. The greatest adjustment to our message was that ***We as men in this country honor our women, and at the very least will wear pink in support of their fight against cancer, all cancer.***

Unlike pink ribbons or bracelets, the wearing of pink shirts by public safety is a highly visible uniformed commitment to our women by men that shows them that we love them, and that we will always be there in their fight against this disease. The pink truck just took it one step further. While on the *Pink Ribbon Tour* I met thousands of people who had been affected by cancer. Of the more than 20,000 women who signed the truck, one-fifth were younger than 30. For many, the truck was a rallying point, a gentle giant that seemed to comfort and inspire everyone from the common citizen to movie stars to government leaders. It truly had the power to heal.

Police and fire departments all over the country were quick to get involved, followed by military leaders and politicians from both sides of the aisle. Some fire departments even painted their reserve trucks pink to use for their own fundraisers, while scores of departments from across the nation emailed telling us how much money they raised for their communities and how great it was wearing their pink shirts. Unfortunately, my own fire department wasn't one of them. To them I was simply employee 06130. Firefighter for the city of Glendale, Arizona.

CHAPTER 5
OUT AT HOME

In baseball, when a batter hits a home run their teammates sometimes give him the silent treatment. It usually happens when a young player is doing well and enjoying a lot of success without having struggled, and the other players want to keep him in check and keep him grounded. After the player hits the home run, and excitedly runs around the bases to the sound of cheering fans, he touches home plate. But no one is there to congratulate him. He quietly picks up his bat and returns to a stoic and silent dugout. No one says a word. There are no pats on the back or even eye contact. His teammates give him the silent treatment for several minutes, and then everyone breaks out and congratulates him and gives him love. It is a rite of passage in baseball. But baseball isn't life.

After the 2008 *Pink Ribbon Tour*, I got the silent treatment from the city of Glendale, from the leadership of the Glendale Fire Department, and from all but a few of the firefighters that I worked with. Most of the guys didn't even ask where I had been; much less acknowledge the program or the pink fire truck. The fire department's silent treatment at the higher level was unjust, but the silent treatment on a baseball diamond *is* just, because players are making light of something grand and then recovering from it. It's delayed acknowledgment, whereas from my perspective, the silent treatment in the department was a ploy to try and smother the program so I would quit the department out of frustration.

To this day, none of the local fire departments has adopted the Cares Enough to Wear Pink Program or has utilized our pink fire trucks to increase awareness of cancer or to benefit its citizens. While I'm on tour the trucks and the program are wildly successful and I can't do enough, but when I come home to the Phoenix area, my trucks are parked because no one asks for them. I had just hit a grand slam for thousands of people with cancer and for women all across the country with no cost to the taxpayers, but in my hometown, I had struck out with the bases loaded and would soon be benched.

Getting love from Jasper.

Hit by the Pitch

When I arrived home from the inaugural *Pink Ribbon Tour* in late October 2008, I immediately returned to work because I had used all my vacation time. One of the conditions that the fire department had imposed upon me prior to the tour was that I keep them informed of everything that I was doing, everywhere I was going, and to notify them of any contact that I might have with the media. I was supposed to let them know every time I got interviewed, what I said, who I spoke with, in which newspaper or magazine the interview would appear, or on which radio or television station it would air, to include all times and dates. It was set up that I was supposed to check in regularly because it was the first year of my program, and because the city didn't know how it would go. But I also believe that it was a set-up. There was virtually no way I could report back to them every time I got interviewed. I was in a no-win situation.

During my final *Pink Ribbon Tour* event at the Sycuan Casino Fire Department outside of San Diego, I was interviewed for an article in a newspaper that goes out to all the city managers nationwide. The Glendale City Manager read the article but said nothing to me about it. Instead, he took it to my chief, who took it upon himself to write me up for major insubordination. Granted, I had not informed the city manager or the chief of that interview because I was only one day away from coming home, nor had I asked for permission to give the interview. But for most of the tour I had done as they had asked. I had checked in several times and had maintained frequent contact. In fact, they often called me to find out if I had spoken to any media, to ask how the tour was going, or to learn about the next stop. They were acting like they were on my side, which was reassuring at the time, but I think that they were truly worried as a city that one of their own firefighters, who happened to be driving a pink fire truck and selling pink tee shirts, was going to get them in trouble. They were looking at the worst-case scenario and were blind to the huge potential for positive publicity and exposure.

About two months after I got back, the assistant fire chief calls and orders me to come downtown, stating that I'm in trouble. I was shocked and confused. "If you guys don't give me hug or a handshake for a job well done I'm going to be pissed off, because everywhere I went for the past two months I got congratulated and celebrated for a job well done, and when I come back to my own professional family you're going to tell me that I'm in trouble?"

My fire chief didn't have the balls to tell me himself, so he had the assistant chief do it. And of course, I was livid. The day I got written up, I went downtown to the Fire Administration Building across the street from the mayor and city manager's office. The assistant fire chief and my union representative were waiting for me in a small conference room, and they were sitting on the same side of the table holding a thick write-up for major insubordination with my name on it. I looked at my union rep and immediately asked him why he was sitting next to the assistant chief and not on my side of the table. "I pay union dues," I barked. "Shouldn't you be sitting next to me?"

"Dave, just sit down. It's no big deal."

"It is a big deal!" I snapped. "I get called on the

carpet and you're writing me up?"

The write-up blindsided me and was a total farce. Typically, whenever a tax-based organization such as a police or fire department encounter major insubordination, they just assume that the employee is so messed up that they either have psychological problems or chemical dependency problems, and they offer them the Emergency Assistance Program (EAP), where the employee undergoes private counseling provided by an independent counselor. The program is funded by the city, but is not associated with the fire or police departments. The employee acquires a counselor and completes a counseling program before returning to the job. In some cases the employee must complete the program before returning to duty or before becoming eligible for certain duties or promotion. It's similar to when a professional or collegiate athlete tests positive for or gets caught with marijuana, alcohol, or other substances. They are required to undergo "therapy" as a way of paying penance before being welcomed back into the fold. In my case, the counseling would be to determine why I was so screwed up that I could be as insubordinate as I was.

The assistant chief tried to calm me down and assured me that the write-up would simply go in my file for a year and then be thrown away.

"This is a total setup!" I shouted. "This is bullshit! At the Fire Academy, when we talked about the representation of a firefighter in the community, we were taught to always ask ourselves if our words or actions can pass the "headline test," and if they can stand up under public view. Can this pass the headline test?"

The assistant chief didn't answer. "This is what the chief wants," he countered, "And I'm going to do it."

"This is all wrong," I exclaimed. "And it's illegal. This is how Enron went down. I spent my own money to buy a fire truck and I used my own vacation time to do something good, then I come home and my own family writes me up and offers me drug counseling. This won't pass the headline test! I'm going to speak to Grant Woods and ask what he has to say."

A Little Help from my Friends

Grant Woods was the former attorney general of Arizona from 1991-1999, and in 1995, was voted by his peers as the nation's top attorney general. After leaving pubic service he went on to enjoy a successful career as a private attorney, and was a key negotiator in the largest civil settlement in history. He was also a friend and a person whom I considered a guardian angel in the flesh. We met at the Arizona Athletic Club when I was 13, and had played basketball together for years. Over time, we developed a strong friendship, and he became a father figure to me and a valued mentor. More than any other person, I looked up to him and trusted his judgment. The mere mention of his name made the assistant chief nervous.

"You don't have to do that," he said. "The write-up just goes in your file."

I shot back. "You aren't the one getting written up! You're bullying me and I don't like it. I'm going to stand up for myself because there's no way I can live up to all the rules and conditions you set. The next time I do something you're going to write me up again, and when I get two or three major write ups, you're going to fire me."

I left the meeting shaking with rage. I immediately called Grant, who quickly calmed me down and said for me to give him some time to make a few phone calls. In the meantime, I told everybody about getting written up. But people didn't want to hear it. When something like this happens in our department, which is a top-heavy, dictatorial-type organization, people stay away because they are afraid for their careers. They're afraid they won't get promoted or that they won't get overtime. Once the news spread about my write up, a few of the guys even began smearing me, saying that I kept the money that I raised selling tee shirts on the tour for myself. Then false rumors spread through several fire stations that I was only doing this to make money off other fire departments. A guy from one department even went to the media claiming that I was asking fire departments that had adopted my program to give me the money from their organizations. Even some of my own local firefighters heard that I was keeping the money, and once they heard that, it was hard to hear the truth. In fact, my own community of firefighters from Phoenix, Mesa, Tempe, and Chandler knew little or nothing about me. But firefighters across the United States, and in some parts of Iraq, Africa, Europe, and Asia knew me, and vouched that every dime of the money they raised in my program stayed in their own communities. In effect, my reputation was being lynched using the vigilante posse approach, where a wild mob hangs a guy, tries him afterwards, then wonders why they hung an innocent person without any proof just because the loudest screamer said to. It was the worst of times.

Two weeks later, I was still mad and Grant had to calm me down again. He said that the legal process does not work as fast as I work. At the time, I was a 44 years old going on 18, and I was fired up ready for war.

But war never came. Grant called Bob Yen, a labor lawyer, and Sun Devil alumnus, who represented the Fraternal Order of Police, and asked if he would read the letter and determine if the city had any legal grounds to write me up. Bob agreed, and generously donated his time. He then called and asked how I wanted to proceed.

"I'm a tax-based low end of the food chain human being," I explained, "If a response comes from me no one will validate it, but if it comes from a law firm that represents me, and if Grant Woods is willing to put his name on it, it will scare the hell out of them."

The write-up against me was so frivolous that we ignored the initial deadline for my response, but the city did nothing. They seemed to realize that the reprimand was unfounded, and perhaps they were hoping the whole situation would diffuse itself. But this was no check swing. The city had committed, and a fastball was on the way.

On January 29, 2009, I submitted my official written response to the write-up, and shortly thereafter, Yen served the mayor, the city manager, and the fire chief with papers indicating the beginnings of a lawsuit against the city and the fire department. The papers stated that what I did was just and charged that what they did was harassment, bullying, and defamation of character, which created a hostile work environment for me. All this I believed to be true. The following was my response to the city:

"Your written reprimand dated January 9, 2009, states that I do not have a right to grieve or appeal your action, but that I may respond and have my response become a part of this action. My response follows.

On my own time and during my vacations I have acted to create awareness of the suffering of women and families affected by breast cancer. I did so because I wanted to show my personal empathy and support for these women and families and I wanted to encourage others to join in my efforts.

Because I am, and for many years, have been proud to serve my community as a firefighter, it was natural for me to call upon my background and experience as a firefighter in my efforts. I therefore carried the theme of our movement by driving a fire truck across country, a truck that was donated and painted pink by local businesses that supported our efforts. Along our cross-country journey, I encouraged firefighters to "wear pink" to show their support for the women in their communities. I was gratified and deeply moved by their willingness to do so, and to otherwise join me in my efforts.

Businesses and individuals along the way also joined and supported our movement by making contributions that allowed us to continue our journey. But along the way, I was most gratified by the men and women who took time out of their days to come to our rallies and show support for the families whose lives were affected by this terrible disease; and I am grateful to the tens of thousands of people who signed our pink fire truck.

I have tried to conduct myself during my off-duty journey, and in my off-duty efforts, in a way that would bring credit to my profession and my community. I am proud to be a firefighter; I am proud to serve the citizens of Glendale, Arizona; and I am proud to be a resident of this city.

Although I believe my off-duty conduct reflects favorably on my profession, and the community I serve, it was not my intention to portray my off-duty efforts and journey as being for or on behalf of the City of Glendale. I did not portray my journey as one conducted for or at the request of Glendale, because it was not. Nor did I portray it as one undertaken while on Glendale's payroll, because it was not.

The media expressed an interest in many things, including my motivations, the origins of the idea for the trek, the reception of the movement in communities across the country, etc. They also wanted facts about me, about where I was from, and where I was going.

I told them that I was from Glendale, that I am a firefighter, and that I started my journey in Glendale. Those are facts. I did not purport to speak or write in the name of Glendale, nor do I wish to. I was not asked about City of Glendale politics, practices or personalities. Nor was I asked about our Department's firefighting techniques or practices. The media had no interest in such things because my campaign was not about those things. My campaign was about trying to do something good; trying to show women and families who have suffered the heartache of breast cancer that they are not alone in their struggles.

Had I been asked about city politics and personalities or departmental practices, I would not have commented on them because they are not a part of what my off-duty campaign is about. Instead, my campaign is about human dignity, compassion and empathy. I believe I have a right during my off-duty time to express myself about such things. I believe my message and conduct could and would bring credit upon the City of Glendale and my Department, if the City and I wished to allow that to happen.

I do not believe that a letter of reprimand is appropriate merely because I have been identified by the media as being a firefighter and from the City of Glendale. Nor do I believe that the reporting of my profession and city of residence give the Department a right to intrude on my off-duty life by requiring me to report to it every time a reporter or media outlet contacts me about my off-duty activities.

I do not believe my conduct constitutes insubordination or, as the letter of reprimand says: "Major insubordination." And I certainly do not believe that my conduct, which has been applauded across the nation, warrants a referral to the City's Employee Assistance Program so that I might secure "professional support" designed "to help people cope with a variety of personal and work related issues."

Leading an off-duty campaign to awaken an

awareness for the suffering of others would not suggest, in my mind, a need for professional counseling services. I am disappointed that the City and this department seem to equate my off-duty humanitarian efforts to on-duty drunkenness and drug abuse.

To the extent departmental directives attempt to interfere in my off-duty speech and conduct, I believe they are unlawful. I do not believe my off-duty conduct is insubordinate. I do not believe my conduct is "Major insubordination.

I ask that the letter of reprimand be removed from my file and that the Department acknowledge my right to engage in off-duty conduct and to hold myself out as a firefighter..."

The city didn't do anything for about a month, then I received a phone call at work informing me that the fire chief, the assistant fire chief, and the union representative were coming down to the fire station to talk to me. They were coming with their tails between their legs because they had been served. Of course, the visit occurred when my truck was conveniently sent off to training and I was left alone at the fire station, all of which I perceived as more bullying and intimidation. And although I didn't have an opportunity to be represented, I did turn on all the computers and brought up sites online that had fire trucks for sale, so when they came in I was sitting in the captain's office looking for fire trucks. It was harmless fun and a small measure of payback. Then the fire chief peeked his head around the door and meekly says, "Hey Dave, are you mad at me?"

"Yes, I'm mad!" I snapped. "Go write up a 20-year-old kid for drinking on the job or someone who has a real problem! Don't write up a guy who is making you look good!"

We went back and forth for 90 minutes in a contentious but calm manner. Although the chief couldn't understand why I got a lawyer, he wouldn't explain his rationale for the reprimand, nor did he ever acknowledge that he went overboard. We saw things from different angles, and at that point we just agreed to disagree rather than to keep arguing. "No matter what you do, I'll never allow my firefighters to adopt your program or to wear pink shirts," he said flatly. "I just don't believe in what you're doing. In the future, be sure to let the department know when you're going to be on duty and when you're not."

I respected his honesty, and was relieved that the whole issue was now behind us. It would have been a political and public relations nightmare for the city to press the issue. Especially against an employee, who five years earlier, had golfed across the country to raise money for children, and who, at no cost to the taxpayers, had just spent two months of his own vacation time on the road in a pink fire truck increasing awareness about cancer. It wouldn't wash. But I still believe to this day that Elaine Scruggs, the mayor, told the city manager and the fire chief to make the situation go away. And although I had served papers on her, she was the only one on my side, which was a testament to her character. And once she knew that one of the city department heads had done something wrong, it was a call to leadership. One that I believe she answered swiftly and honorably.

The city manager is a politician and disavowed

any knowledge of the write up. He realized that I was supported by several powerful people outside the fire service, and when I got written up by the fire department, he probably didn't think I would go to them. No one in our organization ever challenged authority, and the city thought that I would take whatever medicine they gave me, and like it, and that would be the end of it. But that's how our organization does it. That's how they stifle independent thought. That's how they suppress entrepreneurial spirit. That's how they crush dreams. And that's what happens in America all the time. But not that it mattered really. I had fought city hall and had won. I had hit the most important home run of my life, and soon women from across the country stricken with cancer would be cheering for us to drive up to their homes in a pink fire truck just to give them a hug. So much for the silent treatment.

CHAPTER 6
PINK HEALS

Two months on the road during the 2008 *Pink Ribbon Tour* taught me a lot about cancer, about how the business of charity and philanthropy works, and even more about myself. I learned that the lion's share of the work on tour is spent informing and educating a general public that is woefully unaware of the inefficiency of the giant fundraising mechanisms, and in dispelling myths and misinformation about the terrorist called cancer. Despite the subsequent conflict with the Glendale Fire Department, and trying to launch a national movement to raise cancer awareness with a small infrastructure, no money, and little local support, it was full steam ahead. But I needed more pink.

Ribbons No More

The day after I returned from the 2008 *Pink Ribbon Tour* I was already planning the 2009 tour. The first and most important thing I did was to change the name of the *Pink Ribbon Tour* to the *Pink Heals Tour* to begin dispelling the notion that the program only supported women with breast cancer. Too much time had been spent explaining that the program supported all women with cancer, but that was understandable, because I was driving across America in a pink fire truck plastered with pink ribbons that were firmly associated with breast cancer by the wonderful work of the *Susan G. Komen Foundation*. I then ripped the ribbons off the truck, painted it pink, and named it "Karen," in honor of the woman who had donated the money for it. Unfortunately, Karen contracted lung cancer, and how could I drive a truck bearing her name with pink ribbons on it? So it was fitting that I remove the ribbons in honor of her and in honor all women based on love, not just in recognition of women who had battled or were battling breast cancer.

In the spring of 2009, I purchased a fire truck from James Wessel, the owner of Brindlee Mountain Fire Apparatus in Huntsville, Alabama, thus doubling the size of my enormous fleet of pink fire trucks to two. James had the largest used fire truck dealership in the country and was a devout Christian. He had heard about what we were doing, and he had found two trucks from Bangor, Maine that were being sold at auction. He bought both trucks and offered to sell me one for what he paid for it, which was just over $5000. Lisa and I saved up enough money for the flight, and I flew to Alabama and drove the truck back to Arizona. When I got it back, I painted it pink and named it "Elaine" in honor of Elaine Scruggs, the mayor of Glendale. I didn't name it after her because it gave me an advantage in the community, but because Elaine was literally the only person in city government with clout who stood by my side. Meanwhile, she was diagnosed with breast cancer. Having the truck named after her then held added meaning:

"Of all the people that Dave comes into contact with that either have or had cancer, and

had much more difficult times than me, that he put my name on there is a huge honor. I know going out that no one knows who "Elaine" is. He'll probably meet hundreds of Elaine's that either have cancer or who know someone that has cancer, and they'll feel like it's them ... I've signed it. You can see my name and my writing around my name on the picture. I was honored and quite taken aback when he told me that he made that decision ... It's a name that will go out there and other people identify because of somebody in their lives, and I just represent tens of thousands of women everywhere."

Elaine signs "her" truck.

During the summer of 2009, I took "Karen" and "Elaine" on the inaugural *Pink Heals Tour* and we visited 56 cities in 60 days and made scores of unscheduled stops along the way. Toward the end of the tour, the city of Tyler, Texas gave us "Tonya," which was named after a lady in that community who had died from cancer. Although Tonya was still fire engine red, we drove her with us on the remainder of the tour, but she kept breaking down. After several major problems, we finally got her back to Glendale, where we spent almost a year painting her and trying to find out why she wouldn't run well. We discovered that

Tonya

a simple loose wire near the computer was shorting out parts of the truck. But we eventually got her ready and took three trucks on the 2010 *Pink Heals Tour*, which had been expanded to include 78 cities in 74 days. During that time, I got the flu twice and slept in 62 hotel rooms. The greatest thing about it was the people. We didn't have to pay for permits, and when we showed up, cities rolled out the red carpet and footed some of the bill. When my trucks broke down, local business often donated parts and labor.

Pink Heals

And when we needed places to stay, local businesses took the lead and arranged for rooms at a discounted rate or sometimes free. We were almost like traveling gypsies with a pure message, but I kept pushing the envelope. I was getting more time off and the program was getting bigger. It was hard to say no.

All across America people bonded with the trucks on a deeper level than ever before. Giving each a name also gave them a human identity, one that thousands of men and women attending the events could personally connect with. This was driven home during a stop in Park City, Utah, where a man spent 20 minutes photographing "Karen." Finally, as he moved around the truck and stood by the door next to where I was standing, I mentioned that he was "sure taking a lot of pictures of our truck." He then collapsed and began weeping. "My daughter died 10 years ago of cancer," he cried. "And her name was Karen."

I cried with him.

Another time in Burns, Oregon a 67-year-old man and his wife came out of their house to look at the trucks. He had been given two months to live and a friend wanted us to visit him. He came up to the truck with an oxygen tube in his nose and tried to sign it. I could see the pain on his face as he turned to me, "Do you mind if I give you a hug?" I asked. He began tearing up and shaking, so I just hugged him and told him that I loved him. He broke down and so did I. It was a perfect moment. But none of the other guys would go near him because they knew they would lose it too. The following is a note we received from his wife:

"There was an incident that took place in Naperville, Illinois that I'll never forget. A lady

comes up to me and 'Karen', the truck I was driving, and asks if she can put a photo on her. She tells me the story of a 3-year-old old girl that was the daughter of a firefighter that had passed away a month prior due to cancer. I never expected that the stories would be as touching and heartfelt as they were until she came up to me. I'll never forget the look on her face as I taped the picture to the windshield, and as she took photos of it for a keepsake. That's when it hit me just how big the impact we had on everyone. And I'll never forget the passing motorists as we drove on down the freeways. People reaching out their windows, waving, thumbs up, taking pictures. Even at refueling stations we were sharing stories, adding signatures to the trucks. The reactions were amazing. All the different people we encountered at each stop, welcoming us as if we were part of their own."

What Pink Heals is all about.

Pink Heals

Ted Dion, a volunteer driver and full-time firefighter from Coventry, Rhode Island recalls his time on tour:

"Behind the wheel of Elaine, I was able to feel the pride of this organization. I was driving a truck that carried thousands and thousands of well wishes, prayers, memorials, and names of women all over the United States. I was finally part of a team that without a college education or a large amount of money, I could make a difference on a very personal level...Each stop is not predictable and there is no way to calculate the effect of our stop. What I can tell you is what I witnessed firsthand. One of our stops we had been set up for a few hours and doing our routine of sharing love through hugs and caring, when we met a lady who simply came apart while visiting our site. Immediately the tour drivers surrounded her with hugs as she told us, 'My cancer came back today'. I watched big, tough firefighters filled with bravado get filled with tears and love for a total stranger. This is just one of many instances of emotion. I wondered why I was crying, and then at the very moment I realized we are built to love. You really don't have to know someone to love them."

The drivers of the pink fire trucks were an integral part of every tour. Each man had to possess certain qualities and wear several hats, not just that of a firefighter. Each had to be an experienced firefighter or police officer with a commercial driver's license and be willing and able to be away from his family for either 10, 14, or 18 consecutive days, most of which included long, grueling hours on the road. More importantly, each man had to believe in what we were trying to accomplish and be emotionally strong, and yet compassionate, sympathetic, and informed enough about cancer to understand and relate with people battling cancer and with their families. And given the number of breakdowns we experienced, it didn't hurt if they were mechanically inclined and knew how to turn a wrench!

The Pink Heals Tours 2009 & 2010

The 2008 *Pink Ribbon Tour* and the 2009 and 2010 *Pink Heals Tours* were dramatically different, but also similar. Much like brothers and sisters, they had the same parents, were raised in the same environment, but had unique personalities and identities, each replete with good points and bad. They were a collective of individual experiences, shared hardships, and mutual understanding played out in small towns and large cities on a national scale. The myriad stops over the three tours were often difficult and sometimes disappointing, but they were never dull. Although the seemingly endless highway travel could sometimes be numbing, a new adventure always awaited us at the next stop, or as we often encountered, alongside the road in the middle of the night in the form of flat tire or engine trouble. We didn't know if 20 people or 500 would be waiting for us at an event, and if it would be warm and sunny or rainy and cold. But it was that very sense of uncertainty and relentless pushing onward to the next stop to help the women who needed us, that made the tours so challenging and personally rewarding.

Pink Heals

Historically, the tours begin around August 24 of each year and conclude approximately two months later in conjunction with the yearly Cares Enough to Wear Pink Days observance, which is designated from October 25-27. The route of each tour is somewhat determined by the location of the National Fire Chiefs Conference, which we attend. In three short years, the Cares Enough to Wear Pink program and the pink fire trucks have become the top exhibit at the prestigious national meeting.

Following the meeting, the trucks travel a prearranged route making stops at fundraising events, driving in parades, meeting public officials, and visiting fire stations and communities that have adopted the Cares Enough to Wear Pink program or that are being considered for admission as a recognized chapter. But although the tour stops are pre-set, if time allows, we often make unscheduled visits to hospitals, fire stations, private homes, or to wherever we're needed.

Typically, if an event ran long, we would stay overnight in a hotel and travel to the next destination the following day. Occasionally, we would spend a few days in one of the larger cities to take in the sights and to decompress. The mental, emotional, and physical toll is high when living on the road, and dealing with the raw emotion of cancer survivors and those who are battling the disease, is as difficult as it is rewarding. The following two letters reflect this:

"Dave: I just wanted to let you know that my mom rode the fire truck in Wentzville (MO) during the parade and four short days after that she was in the hospital having brain surgery. Her breast cancer has now entered her brain

and there is no cure for it. This is the worst thing I can ever think of and can't imagine my life without my mom. She will always remember the day in the fire truck, you made it special, and for that I will never forget that or you. Thank you for being you and for making a difference in peoples lives. I love you, and I don't even know you. But you put a smile on my face and that is all I need. You are the greatest. –Unsigned."

"I was just diagnosed with breast cancer a couple weeks ago. Seeing this pink fire engine made me smile and cry. I know I now have a battle ahead of me but I know it is one I can win! Seeing so many people out there being supportive of this great cause makes me feel like I know that I ...along with everyone else will have a great chance to fight and win! Thank you, Gail."

Jasper has a ticket to ride.

Pink Heals

Once at an event, the fire trucks were parked and we would introduce ourselves and explain why we were there. Sometimes that included explaining the entire Cares Enough to Wear Pink program, and other times we were simply part of a larger rally and offered support through our trucks. At most events we set up a table and sold Cares Enough to Wear Pink tee shirts as the ONLY way of paying for our fuel and other expenses on the road, such as truck repairs, tolls, and food and lodging when needed. But we accepted NO money for ourselves or for the Cares Enough to Wear Pink program, and that's why the program has grown in size, respect, and in support from fire chiefs, politicians, city managers, and citizens alike. There have been over 30 events where people have marched up on a stage and handed me a check for thousands of dollars, but I refused all of them. I would then warn everyone to be leery of a person who walks into their community and promises the world for a price, because more often than not, that person will steal them blind and leave nothing for when a real tragedy occurs. Sadly, that happened in several communities I visited, and I had to rebuild trust and inspire new hope, which was never easy. Our aim was to selflessly help communities inspire their own people to take care of their own people, not to take advantage or to diminish. That has been and will always be the core message of the Cares Enough to Wear Pink program.

Strangely, convincing people to adopt a program to help their own can be a tough sell. Cancer is ugly, and most people who aren't directly affected by it don't want to face it. And understandably so. But that won't make it go away. For many, it is easier to care from a distance by writing a check and donating from afar rather than giving the money directly to a person who is suffering from cancer. We need generous people and their heroic efforts, but we also need to stop throwing money around just because we don't want to stare cancer in the face. Much of the money donated to cancer research is spent on the overhead costs associated with raising the money, and not on treating the patient. We've got to do an about face, stare cancer down, and find a cure.

One great difference between the *Pink Ribbon Tour* and the *Pink Heals Tours* was that no one could tell me "no" while on the latter trip. During the *Pink Ribbon Tour*, it was empowering traveling across the country knowing that I was doing the right thing by selling a message to help fight breast cancer, but that same message also gave everyone an opportunity to say "no" to the program if they're weren't personally affected by it. But beginning with the first *Pink Heals Tour*, our message changed from one of breast cancer awareness to one of celebrating our own communities and taking care of our women first. No one could say "no" to that.

When I toured the country for breast cancer in 2008, everybody without breast cancer said, "Way to go, Dave, but my wife doesn't have breast cancer. What can you do for her?"

The questions were valid and I quickly realized that the larger issue was battling ALL diseases that threatened women. On the *Pink Heals Tour* and with our organization now, whether a woman has breast cancer or not, we are wearing her shirt to let her know that she is loved. Then, if she or anyone in her family gets cancer, we help. Of course, many people still do

The new Pink Heals logo dedicated to battling testicular cancer. The slogan is in honor of Jarret White, a testicular cancer survivor and Glendale firefighter, who gave me the idea.

not make the distinction, but I'm kicking down the walls of misunderstanding and our chapters are spreading a larger message. Frequently, women say to me, "My husband has testicular cancer, and no one ever helps people with testicular cancer. What can you do about that?" Then another woman will overhear her and say, "Do you understand that these pink trucks represent every human being? They just put our women first like we all should."

People who have been educated about the Cares Enough to Wear Pink program are now uniting to educate those who don't understand the program or who won't research it for themselves. These people are fighting back for me, so I often don't have to say a word. They have become the warriors, the teachers, and the ambassadors of the program, and together

Nicki Janne & Josh Baker.

we are rapidly implementing a new way to brand the way that love, hope, support, and synergy are wielded in communities across the county. We have planted the seeds, and they are growing, and soon the women of America will be reaping the harvest. The movement is growing exponentially and appeals to all demographics. It is neither religious nor politically based, and definitely is not corporately run. The Cares Enough to Wear Pink program has made a dramatic impact in the lives of thousands. People are leaving their traditional cancer and charitable organizations to support the trucks, because we are not all about money, we are about people. We qualify events by asking the organizers if we can bring pink fire trucks to their walks or other events, but they often say no. The main reason that I have not significantly interacted with *Susan G. Komen* and the American Cancer Society is that I sell tee shirts to raise money for my fuel and expenses, and they believe that would take away from their own fundraising bottom line, which is fine. But the trucks are more than a fundraising tool and a bottom line to the people who sign them. For people with cancer, signing the trucks is a symbolic act in a lengthy and bitter struggle against a disease that ultimately might kill them. To others, it honors family and friends who have lost the battle. But to all, the trucks represent hope and serve as rallying points to keep the fight against a deadly disease alive. The people who sign and support the trucks are better representatives of love, caring, and hope than any dollar ever raised on a walk.

One of the most important things I learned from the 2008 *Pink Ribbon Tour* is that men in this country are some of the greatest human beings on earth.

I met men who truly love their wives and who have cried every day since losing them to cancer. I met grandfathers who have cashed in their retirements and sold everything so their grandchildren could receive the cancer treatment they needed. I met fathers who had the courage to wake up every day, work hard, and sacrifice everything for the women and children they loved. Men with limitless heart and infinite love who were trying to protect their families and trying to make a difference the best way they knew how. In these men, I saw heroism at its most basic but exalted level. Most never wore a uniform.

A moving scene at a KC chapter event.

The love for women that I witnessed moved me deeply, but it was not until we were invited to Bartlett, Illinois that I fully understood and appreciated the importance of women, not just in our country, but around the world. Following the local fire chief and others, we arrived at a Hindu temple that is among the largest and most beautiful temples outside India. Since photography was not allowed inside, several photographers and PR people photographed our fire truck in front of the temple. Afterward, we went in, removed our hats and shoes, and put on robes out of respect. We were then given a private tour, which blew everyone away. The temple was made from limestone obtained in Turkey, and from fine marble found in Italy. Each piece was hand carved in India and then shipped to Bartlett, and assembled in just 16 months by over 1700 volunteers from the Chicago area. The temple contains thousands of tiny figurines of women in gold, silver, and bronze in different poses hanging from the ceiling and walls. Our guide told us many devotees commit to the temple, and that several live their entire lives there. I told my new Hindu friend that Donald Trump could not pay the best laborers in the world a million dollars a minute to produce the quality of workmanship found in that temple. He agreed:

> *"Our religion doesn't recruit, and it doesn't try to grow in membership. All our religion teaches is love through women. Many of the principal figures in Hinduism are women. Why do you think we brought your fire truck here? You could have a billion dollars and not touch the number of lives that you have touched with that fire truck. Money couldn't buy your truck because it's based on love."*

His words were profound and moved me deeply. Until that day, I hadn't truly understood what I had created or who I was. I was still Dave the pitcher, and I was just out there firing fastballs. I just loved playing in the game for whatever reason, but I didn't understand the game, much less appreciate it. From that point on, I became forward thinking about the pink fire trucks and about what I could actually accomplish without selling my soul.

Out of the News

The Hindu temple in Bartlett, Illinois.

The greatest void in all three tours was the lack of national media exposure. When I traveled the country on tour and spoke to groups of fifty to five thousand people about the *Pink Heals Program*, I was bombarded with the same questions over and over, "Why haven't you been on the Oprah Show?" or "Why haven't you been on the Ellen Show?" or "Why haven't you been on the Today Show?" Why? Why? Why?

Simple. I was not corporate driven or financed. There was no gain for the networks to publicize the program other than for ratings, and I wasn't the Super bowl or Dancing with the Stars. Another reason that the national media has avoided the program is because it lacks a well-known front man or famous spokesperson. But no paid spokesperson is as passionate about the program or as driven as I am, and if we hired a spokesperson, he or she wouldn't be doing it for the right reasons, nor would they have the same impact. They'd only be doing it to collect a fee, and until it's just for a job well-done, it will always be for the wrong reasons. Unless it's community minded, and I get one person to spearhead the program like it's their own, most communities will adopt the program just because I'm coming to town in a pink truck and because they don't want to let their own women down. Once this book gets into circulation, I will get to

A hug and a smile.

speak on my own thought process of why I do what I do based on the inspiration I have for everybody, and because it's in my nature to help and protect people. Then everyone will listen and say, "I could do that." Let's hope so.

Pink Heals on Mother's Day

Beginning in May 2011, I expanded the *Pink Heals Tour* to include a Mother's Day Mini-Tour. From May

Pink Heals

3 to June 12, 2011 the tour was launched throughout California, Utah, and Oregon. It included 18 scheduled and six unscheduled stops in 14 cities with the purpose of introducing the Cares Enough to Wear Pink program into new areas, paying personal visits to newly established chapters, and revisiting loyal friends. The mini-tour was an inevitable outgrowth of the traditionally longer *Pink Heals Tour* and served as a testing ground for new trucks, drivers, and equipment.

Fresno & Clovis Police & Fire Departments during a tour of California. Our Pink Heals Tour drivers are on top of the trucks.

It was also important because it reemphasized that our organization is by no means exclusively about breast cancer, and reminded people that the color pink is the representation of all women. We did the tour to honor mothers and their family members battling cancer, and to reaffirm that we are celebrating the glue in our communities and what they mean to us.

Pink Heals

The turnout and enthusiasm for the events ranged from low in Southern California where the program is new, to very strong as we traveled north through the state and into Oregon and Utah where the program had already gained a foothold through previous tours. And although the tour was a success, I was reminded of the work that I had left to do and how difficult it would be. But the tour also reaffirmed my instinct to follow my passion and my heart, and to not go out of my way to make people happy or to let them do the same with me. In the non-profit world, I meet people in a genuine light, and they want to help so they can feel good about themselves. In doing so, they often promise what they cannot deliver. I understand and accept that this comes with the territory, but as a former relief pitcher that was called upon to perform under pressure and to close out big

Games, I also realize that the ultimate goal is to win regardless of how ugly the fashion, rather than to lose while looking good. Armed with that reaffirmation,

Guardians having fun in Sonoma.

Pink Heals

I promise that as long as I am able to drive a pink fire truck down the highways of America to deliver a hug to a woman in need, that will never happen.

Down Time

After returning from any tour, I have to relax for a few days, and although it's not my nature to reflect or dwell on the past, I can't help but to think of Leslie Hulse, a police officer whom I met in Fishers, Indiana during the 2009 *Pink Heals Tour*. Leslie was dying of cancer and we visited her at home in our pink truck wearing our pink turnouts to give her a hug. Her parents told us that this was the first time she had smiled in weeks, and they agreed to put her in a wheelchair and to wheel her out to sign her name on the truck before she died. Leslie bravely signed the truck and even allowed us to videotape her story, which can be viewed on our website. Sadly, Leslie lost her courageous battle on September 28, 2009, but she is not forgotten. We now have a truck named, "Leslie," which is our fourth. Her story and hundreds like it moved me in a profound way and reaffirmed my belief that whenever we lift up someone who is down, we elevate ourselves to do even more. My mission is clear.

Jen Kelly (left) and Leslie Hulse.

CHAPTER 7
GRASS ROOTS

Now that I have explained the history of the *Cares Enough to Wear Pink/Pink Heals Program*, it's time to get busy mending America. After all, isn't this what the book is about? Fixing what is broken and saving our country from terrorists and regaining our status as the wealthiest, most powerful, most educated, and most advanced nation in the world? Well, sort of. But an individual can only do so much to reduce the national debt or increase the efficiency of the military, or even raise our children's math and science scores to compete with the rest of the world. Sure, one motivated individual might make a small impact in one of those areas, but what about terrorism? More than being vigilant and consenting to searches at the airports, each individual can help stop terrorism. No, not the Taliban or Al Qaeda or the scores of other terrorist groups. This terrorist has killed more people than any of them and has caused more deaths than all of our wars combined. It is the most lethal, insidious, and destructive terrorist that we face today. It is indiscriminate and recognizes no difference among the education, social status, or station of its victims. It impartially kills young and old, male and female, rich and poor. The terrorist is cancer. But there is hope. And it can be found in all of us.

Women First

The Cares Enough to *Wear Pink/Pink Heals Program* is for everyone and can be implemented at the grass roots level in virtually any town or city in America. It is both proactive and restorative, and begins with the philosophy that we put the women of our community first. These are our mothers, wives, sisters, and daughters, and if a man cannot put them first, he is not a man. We also recognize and honor our women and the color pink, which represents them. It is their color and we recognize the love they give and their power to heal. Pink heals all wounds.

But we are self centered. We think only about our taxes, our gasoline prices, our jobs, our stock market, and our 401Ks. They're all going away, and we don't know where the money is going. This program is about our community, our family, our neighbors, and our leaders, and how it will help bring us back together to focus on our own people now, rather than on promises that were never kept, opportunities that were lost, and things that might have been. Pink will heal as long as we do it in service to our women and what they mean to us in our communities, not just because they are sick or stricken with cancer. Because if we use illness as the sole motivation for action, once the sickness is gone, so is our cause for coming together, and we ultimately revert to the same dysfunctional state. Our organization is about embracing our own people and our own communities. It's about when a house burns down and the neighbors help rebuild it because they are part of the community. We don't watch our neighbor's house burn down, then walk into our own house and say, "I hope they had insurance." It's about developing the mindset that we are interconnected and interdependent, and that charity truly begins at home in our own community. In today's society, we do not want to acknowledge others' catastrophe because we don't want to assume the responsibility of helping to repair or rebuild. If we inspire people to approach those who are hurting, even in their own homes, and acknowledge that we love them, and reassure them that we're starting over again, and that we won't give up, we have begun the healing and restorative process. It's akin to a modern day barn-raising where tragedy is acknowledged and the burden of rebuilding is shared.

Evan Littlejohn getting a hug from a survivor.

One of the people I most admire is Simon O. Sinek, the renowned marketing consultant who developed "The Golden Circle" model based on human decision making. He's a wonderful speaker, and he often talks about why 250,000 people attended Martin Luther King's famous rally in Washington DC. Sinek contends that most of the people did not come to hear King speak. Instead, they came because they bought into his belief system and into his passion, and that they went to make themselves feel good. They understood King's message and why he was doing it, but the buy-in was to feel good about themselves. And that's where the *Pink Heals Program* begins, the belief system that Pink heals everything. That is the "why." But words and belief systems are nothing without action.

The Pink Heals Program

The *Cares Enough to Wear Pink/Pink Heals Program* is simple and free. But, it's not easy. It is a community-based effort organized and run by local individuals, typically employees from fire and/or police departments or any other tax based agency, who organize fundraising events and produce and sell clothing bearing the *Cares Enough to Wear Pink*/Pink Heals logo, and re-distribute the money directly back into their community as they see fit. There is no cost to

The guys from Bismarck, North Dakota.

the community, its citizens, or to its public employees. Nor are there any sign-up fees, membership dues, or administrative costs associated with becoming a *Pink Heals Program*. However, each *recognized chapter* is ultimately required to acquire a fire truck and to paint it pink. Most trucks are in used condition, and are either donated or purchased independently through proceeds garnered through fundraisers, or obtained through private donations. To maintain uniformity in our trucks, we supply the pink paint and the logos after prospective chapters have completed a number of steps proving that they are serious and capable of running a Pink Heals chapter.

The response to the program has been incredible. Sixteen months ago, we had three pink fire trucks and no active chapters. Today, we have 34 local Pink Heals chapters with over 40 pink fire trucks on the road, and several more in various stages of completion. However, interest in the Pink Heals movement is not just limited to the United States. In 2010, firefighter John Power formed *Guardians Le Ribbon Pink Heals* chapter in Montreal, Canada, and is busy working on more. Although the name and mission statement was tweaked a little to comply with Canadian law, the logos remain the same, and the chapters are still based on our model. Firefighters in the Philippines, Australia, South Africa, Iraq, Germany, and in the Philippines, have also expressed strong interest, while queries have been received from fire chiefs in Italy and Brazil. Pink fire trucks and other public service vehicles, are increasingly being developed in this country and in others, and our goal is to have over 100 trucks on the road.

Getting Started

For anyone interested in organizing a *Cares Enough to Wear Pink*/Pink Heals chapter, first do your homework. Put in the research. Invest the time. Expend the energy. Then be honest. Is the program right for you and your community? Are you right for it? Do you have the time and energy to commit? Now is the time to ask questions. Go to the Pink Heals Tour Facebook page at *www.facebook.com/PinkHealsTour* or visit our website at *www.pinkfiretrucks.org*. Read the testimonials. Look at the photos. Watch the videos. And make an honest evaluation. Ask yourself if this is something you really want to do. If so, contact me by email and let's get started!

Chapter by Chapter

One clear distinction must be made. A Pink Heals chapter is not part of a public fire or police department. Rather, it is an organization using a fire truck driven by off-duty firefighters, typically, to serve their community. We are building a completely new program that is separate from fire and police and separate from politicians and churches, but one that consists largely of off-duty public safety personnel who wish to do more.

When we first created the *Pink Heals Program*, we designated some of the first applicants as a chapter of a specific community or county. As we formed more chapters, we also faced growing pains. Some chapters that were in close proximity did not want to share geographic areas. This was especially problematic in communities in the east, where densely populated boroughs were often separated only by railroad tracks.

There might be a dense area of 50,000 people within a ten square mile area, and then nothing for twelve miles, then another town of 15,000 people, and so on down the line. My initial idea was to have a chapter in every small community, whether it was a 25-square mile area or a 100-square-mile area, which was easy to do in parts of Texas, where a hundred miles or more might separate communities. Although currently, there is no set policy, in the future we are looking at awarding chapters based on the congressional model where population determines how much representation is needed. At 8 a.m., on any given day, if there were a thousand pink fire trucks driving down the road a million women would know they're loved, but if one chapter carries half of a state, there is no way they could get enough trucks on the road to spread the message to more people. For instance, if the program were suddenly to take hold in the Phoenix area, I could not perform adequately enough to validate my program. I would need more trucks and more help, but I do not want either. I want other chapters to take on more responsibility and to own their own trucks. I don't have a lot of support within my own community, and often I have to enlist people on a Saturday night to come with me to deliver flowers to a woman with cancer, but when I leave my community on tour, the whole country embraces the organization.

There are chapters that also have difficulty getting their communities to embrace their program, but by us touring the country, we validate their trucks so their community supports them. We give them a million dollars worth of marketing by doing it the way we do it. All they have to do is to stay true to the program, stay simple, and serve their community with their pink fire truck. Their job is not to create new art or new logos, it is to help people.

Leadership

Without good leadership and direction there is little chance of success in anything, and identifying concerned, capable, and committed leadership is a vital step in establishing a local *Cares Enough to Wear Pink*/Pink Heals chapter. The leader of a Pink Heals chapter should be a can-do person who is or has been part of the fire service or who has an interest or connection with it. A good leader should be someone who works well under pressure, can multi-task, and be a person who leads from the front by example rather than from an easy chair from the rear.

Although it is helpful to enlist local tax-based and civic leaders, it is not essential. Just because a person holds a leadership role, does not guarantee they are a good leader. True leadership puts the needs and welfare of those being led first, while judiciously balancing the realities of limited resources and manpower capabilities with expectations and wants. The following are seven principal manpower pools from where potential leadership should be drawn: police officers, firefighters, mayors, city managers, city council members, women's auxiliaries, and healthcare professionals. However, great care should be taken when considering whether leadership of a *Pink Heals Program* is realistic. Ideally, the person should be an experienced leader, and have a background in the military, in public safety, or have been a leader or manager in education or in the business world.

Leadership is not easy and the burden is sometimes heavy, but for a selfless and motivated person who is dedicated to making a difference in peoples' lives, the personal satisfaction is immense.

Our job as leaders is to give the program away to our own community, let them take credit for it, and then to celebrate our women and what they mean to us in our lives, not because they have cancer. Communities that get it right empower their leaders to get involved in the program. But first, they have to earn their wings.

In Writing

It is said that an oral contract is only as good as the paper it is written on. That may be true, but once a prospective chapter applies for membership, they must sign an agreement promising to abide by certain rules and to follow the general policies and procedures of the Guardians of the Ribbon, Inc. This includes filing corporate non-profit paperwork for their own city, and acquiring their own tax ID so they can pay tax on the merchandise they sell. As a 501(c)(3) non-profit organization, it is imperative that each chapter fully comply with all federal laws relative to the corporation, and to observe all mandates. Don't get me wrong, I loved breaking rules and bucking city hall as much as the next person, but breaking federal law whether knowingly or not, is inexcusable.

The next mandatory step is that each chapter be able to perform and to prove leadership by meeting their mayor, their city government, their tax-based groups, their city council, and to get the community to adopt the program in writing as a fund-raising mechanism for their city with nothing in it for themselves. Once their community has adopted the program, the prospective chapter is given the okay to purchase a fire truck.

The greatest challenge facing any chapter and its members is staying grounded once they have a truck, and remembering that they are the same people as they were before they got the truck. We have a chapter that gets one truck and immediately starts thinking about how to acquire another. Their focus should be about delivering flowers to a woman newly diagnosed with cancer and giving her a hug, not building more trucks. Granted, pink trucks are impressive. However, as an organization, we do not want people getting home equity loans and getting into financial straits just because they want a pink fire truck or want to increase their fleet. A chapter can be formed without a truck, and initially should focus on the core message of the program, which is raising money to help fight cancer in their own community. We have chapters whose firefighters have several trucks but do not have enough money for fuel because they ignored the essential fundraising side of the program. If the chapters don't have enough money for fuel, they don't drive to a woman's home. They sell some tee shirts and make the money they need. It's either about the money or about the service. If we stay in service to others, it's never about the money.

Driving to be the Best

The chapters that are the most successful are those whose chapter heads have traveled with me on tour. Because of this, we have now made it mandatory that any person wanting to become a chapter must have its principal officer sign up to be a driver and accompany

Official Proclamation of the State of Arizona.

me on tour for at least ten days. Through this trial by fire process, we have trained many outstanding chapter heads who have a clear understanding of the program and the level of commitment needed to make it work. There is no messing around and we take the job seriously. By accompanying me on a national tour, the leaders actually see and hear the message delivered in real time, not on the computer or in print. They get to feel the synergy being created with the audience and to experience the impact of touching lives up close and personal. It's like doing live theater, creating in the moment, and becoming part of something greater than the sum of its parts. Armed with that understanding, experience, and emotion, drivers return home with an established and proven operational model, and a lifetime of memories to draw upon.

The Art of Pink

Beginning in 2007-08, Lisa designed the first Cares Enough to Wear Pink tee shirts for the 2008 *Pink Ribbon Tour* as a way of paying for our fuel and travel expenses. We now have 12 different tee shirt designs and we are constantly designing new shirt-art to keep our shirts fresh and relevant, because when the national tour comes through a city, we want to have great looking shirts that people want to buy. If we return to a community two or three years in a row, we want a different shirt each year. No one wants to buy the same shirt because they already have one, and it's by the sale of these shirts and other apparel, that we keep our trucks moving. Any new art that Lisa creates, the national chapter uses it exclusively for three months before releasing it to the chapters.

The job of the local fire departments and local chapters, once they have been approved as chapters, is to give the art away to their community leaders and to let them take the ball and run with it. That means everybody wins and no one loses. As long as the chapters adhere to a few common sense guidelines, such as not using profanity, distasteful or offensive language, or depicting anything that represents drugs, nudity, or anything illegal, they can design and tailor their clothing to fit the character of their community and fire departments. The goal is to sell the shirts to people who want to support and empower our women in their fight against all cancers.

Four years after designing her first tee shirt, Lisa's creations have gone global. Pink Heals Apparel has exploded in popularity and women all over the world are buying her clothing items bearing the *Cares Enough to Wear Pink*/Pink Heals logo because they trust us. Lisa experiments with the colors, the art, and with different styles of clothing, and handles the entire retail operation. She has the clothes made, takes the orders, and ships the merchandise, with all profits going to support our trucks.

Me (left) and the crew selling shirts on tour.

As the program grows, our long-range strategic goal is to create a clothing line based on our value system as an organization, and to establish "Pink Heals Apparel" retail stores or kiosks in every city that we have a pink fire truck. Women in each community would buy jeans, panties, bras, purses, belts, skirts, blouses, and anything else that a typical clothing store would have for women, and the net proceeds generated would go to non-profit organizations and to people in that community battling cancer. Hundreds of stores across the country will generate money for their own communities, and people can support their own people by purchasing items they commonly use. The stores are simply the next evolutionary step in the *Pink Heals Program*.

Infrastructure

To effectively support any legitimate charitable organization or program, it helps to have a solid infrastructure staffed with experienced and motivated people. It's important to understand and clearly define the roles, responsibilities, and expectations for each person in the Pink Heals organization without limiting or restricting them to specific aspects of the operation. Non-profit and charitable organizations are manned and staffed by many caring, dedicated, and capable people who have their own personal reasons for volunteering their service, and it is essential that their talents, abilities, and contributions be maximized without overburdening them. But, it is also necessary to insure that everyone is trained and experienced in several facets of the program so it can continue to operate smoothly if, for whatever reason, someone is unavailable or unable to perform their duties. This also fosters a sense of teamwork and solidarity that is the lifeblood of any organization.

Another element of a solid infrastructure is to utilize existing channels of support. In other words, are there any existing sources for free manpower, facilities, equipment, or are there any political, media, or social pipelines that can be tapped to assist in fundraising efforts? Are there opportunities to combine forces with other organizations that share a common goal? The collective power of like-minded people can be amazing, but only if they are tuned in and aware of what the other organization needs. Like so many other effective programs, communication is paramount in developing potential sources to expand the program.

While corporations are a potentially huge source of support for the *Cares Enough to Wear Pink/Pink Heals Program* and can offer a strong and ready-made fundraising infrastructure, there are often too many strings attached. I avoid corporate sponsorship and do not solicit donations from them. I want to support the organization through a clothing line that is driven by our passion to take these trucks and change the world, and change how we view people who are sick. People will buy our clothes specifically for that, not because they know the money is going for research. They're giving me money knowing the why.

Model Chapters

Our first Pink Heals chapter was Hinesville, Georgia and is headed by Shane Shifflett, a military firefighter at nearby Ft. Stewart, and a driver on the first *Pink Heals Tour*. Shane and his chapter have four fire trucks and a police car and have done an outstanding job. His trucks all look like chapter trucks and the logos all look like the logos that are supposed to go on the trucks. He doesn't deviate from the rules. If we're taking the money and just acquiring trucks and we're not performing the mission within the community, we would be chastised, but he's taken the program and rolled.

211

Shane & Denise Shifflett & their truck "Mary."

The chapter headed by Ryan McMurray in Washington Courthouse, Ohio is another exemplary chapter. The chapter doesn't have a lot of money or people, but the people they do have are close knit and operate within their means. They are selfless humanitarians, outstanding human beings, and a credit to their profession. They are not about going out and soliciting money. They are all about people.

The preeminent chapter in the entire program belongs to Ted Dion, the Rhode Island Chapter president from Coventry. Ted rode with me on tour to learn about my program so he could start it in his own community, which he did. His organization is on fire and performs like no other. The people and firefighters in his community love him because he has his finger on the pulse of the people, and because of this, the community has embraced his truck more than any other truck in the country. He is totally vested in the success of the program and goes the extra mile. His firefighters are constantly finding new ways to better the lives of women in their community and frequently deliver roses in their pink truck to women diagnosed with cancer. To show the character of his men, while Ted was on the road with me learning the ropes and doing everything he was required to do, they were secretly building a fire truck to present to him in honor of his mom who had cancer. They were in frequent contact with me working out the details of the truck, and when he returned, his men presented him with a finished ladder truck. Pink of course.

Ted Dion (upper left) in procession. The cars are pink too!

These are just a few of the outstanding chapters that are part of the *Cares Enough to Wear Pink/Pink Heals Program*. Each in its own way brings something unique and special to the program, and collectively serves to strengthen the movement through their fundraising and promotional efforts. Without the hundreds of dedicated volunteers that make up the program, thousands of women suffering with cancer would not receive the care and support they currently enjoy. But there is always one more thing to do. One more thing that can be done better. One more person to save. It all begins at the grass roots level with dedicated people reaching out to help those less fortunate and enlisting the help of even more people to keep the circle of life turning in the right direction.

(L-R) Scott Phillips, me, Steve Cannon. Scott and Steve are captains on the Glendale Fire Department and long-time friends and supporters. Behind us is the oldest fire truck in our fleet, a 1952 Ford, owned by John Lovie, our Napa Valley chapter.

Going Rogue

Most volunteers in the Pink Heals organization are outstanding people with enormous hearts and a selfless desire to help others. And some are not. No organization is perfect, and that was best illustrated by one of our members who went rogue and violated every principle the organization stands for. As the head of the program, it is my responsibility to insure that the people we enlist are solid, but I was lax in my duty and failed to do a thorough background check on one person because I was excited and anxious that he wanted to join the movement. One of my faults is that I always think that people have the same value system and integrity that I do. Boy, was I wrong!

When I first met Bob, (not his real name), at the annual International Association of Fire Chiefs Conference in Dallas in 2009, I was impressed. He came across as a hard-working blue-collar gentleman who asked all the right questions and had a great sense of humor. He had built a truck, which he called his 9-11 Tribute Truck, in honor of all the men and women who died in 9-11, and had it covered with plaques bearing the name of each individual. Since he was at the conference, I just assumed he was credible. He then approached me and asked what it would take to start a chapter in Dallas. I naively said, "Just get a truck and paint it pink and follow our lead."

That's how easy it was. Bob went out and soon got a pink fire truck, quickly followed by another. But it wasn't long before we started getting hints from people in the community that he was going out of state to Louisiana, and building a $40,000 military truck for a child who was dying of brain cancer. Later, we learned that he got an entire community to attend a fundraiser to pay the money for the truck, and then got them to paint it pink. Even worse, after the fundraiser he did not give the people the title to the truck and wanted to take it back to Dallas with him.

Bob was a conman. We later found out that he didn't have a title or insurance on his pink fire truck nor did he even have a driver's license. We also discovered that he had spent a year in prison, and that he had been disowned by his siblings and by his elderly parents, who both suffered with cancer. He was driving around in a pink truck that we validated, and almost overnight he became the disenfranchised son of his parents to a local hero, and he was basking in the credibility and validation he received from women by selling tee shirts that he was running through his son's PayPal account.

It wasn't long before I received a call from the owner of the military truck asking for the title. I didn't know anything about it. I had told Bob not to build a military truck by himself, but to inspire the family and the local community to build and take ownership of their own military truck, but he did it anyway. He ignored my repeated attempts to help and continued to say and do his own thing. That is, until I had enough.

After about 18 months, Bob was removed from our program. Our accountant then removed him from our internet chapter page and notified the IRS that he was eliminated from the chapter altogether. Ultimately, his truck was impounded and Bob hasn't been heard from since, and as a result of his action, extensive background checks are now completed on each potential member.

The Bottom Line

My philosophy of life is simple and comes from baseball: If I perform and I am successful, then the crowd will eventually celebrate me, and in turn, I will get paid. The same philosophy can be applied to the *Pink Heals Program*. If chapters and organizations work hard, give away the program for free, and get their communities to adopt it, they will raise more money to give to the organizations that serve the community. Then of course, these large, pink trucks will start getting donations from local businesses and more people will be served.

The *Pink Heals Program* is unlike any other program. We do not put ourselves in a pretty pink uniform just to tell everybody how good we are when we haven't performed. Wherever we speak, people want to give us money, but we tell them that they are only giving us money based on the spoken word, not on performance. Make us perform. Quit giving us money without a just reason. Yes, I threw strikes. Yes, I struck the guy out. Yes, we won the game. And yes, I earned the money. If I pull into a town a thousand miles away and someone buys a tee shirt, they give me the money and the deal is done. There are no promises made that I can't keep. They get what they paid for. We don't solicit sponsors, but if someone donates money to a chapter, they can accept it as long as it remains in their own community.

I can inspire people to give me money, but I don't. That's what corporate charity does. They convince people and their businesses to fundraise and to donate money for hope, but instead, it pays a lot of salaries and a lot of people, while back in that community where the money was generated, people are sick and can't get help. I believe that people should be giving the money directly to their own local demographic and to their own local charities.

On our website, we do not ask for donations. We only ask that people buy Pink Heals clothing if they are interested, because their sale helps keep the trucks running. Approximately 30,000 communities have adopted the program in four years, and they are fundraising to help their own people. No one does what we do. A good example would be if we were Nike, which is a huge for-profit company, and we gave every other company in the country free instructions how to build our sneakers. Then we give them "Michael Jordan" and the famous "Swoosh" icon, and say, "Please take 100 percent of the money you earn from it and give it to women with cancer in your own area." The *Pink Heals Program* is "Nike." Our fire trucks are "Michael Jordan," and our art and our movement are the "Swoosh." That's why the *Pink Heals Program* is growing like wildfire. People get a great product for free and it helps everyone.

In 2009, the IAFF (International Association of Firefighters), which is about 350,000 members strong, adopted the program, so everywhere there is a union fire shop there is a Cares Enough to Wear Pink program. So each fire department is wearing our slogan, wearing our shirts, selling those shirts and donating the money to local charities that are helping families battling cancer. Beyond that, the state legislature of Oklahoma adopted it, so the whole state of Oklahoma is caring enough to wear pink, and it keeps growing. Florida adopted it, Texas adopted it, and before the union adopted it, we were already in 38 states. Dave Graybill, employee #06310. If I can do it, you can too.

Pink Heals Chapter Checklist

The following is a simple checklist reminder on how to start your own Pink Heals chapter and begin raising money for your community:

1. You - Contact us by email or phone stating your interest.
2. We - Speak to you and evaluate you for the program.
3. We – Send you an application & Agreement.
4. You – Read, understand, sign, & return it to us.
5. We – Do a background check.
6. You – Go to the city and get them to adopt the Program in writing. & You Sign up as a driver & do a stint on tour.
7. We – Accept you as a chapter & send you free tee shirt art.
8. You – Make & sell your own tee shirts and acquire a fire truck.
9. We – Send you the free paint.
10. You – Have the truck painted and begin making a difference!

Pink Heals

Grass Roots

CHAPTER 8
THE POWER OF PINK

I hate the status quo—especially when it isn't working—and I love Einstein's quote that "Insanity is doing the same thing, over and over again, and expecting different results." Politically, our country is insane, and that insanity has spilled over into every facet of our lives, and if we're not careful and vigilant, it will wash us away. I'm not calling for revolution or advocating that our system of government be changed, only the "insane" parts that don't work. Instead of returning to the same dry well day after day, let's dig a new one. Let's discard the terms "traditional, conservative, liberal, and entitlement" and exchange them for "common sense, performance, service, accountability, and leadership," just to name a few. Let's begin growing our leaders locally and taking care of our communities first. Let the ripple effect begin at home and spread outward rather than the other way around. Make all leadership, not just elected or appointed, performance based and hold it immediately accountable. Let's not take the "everybody gets a medal" or "participation award" approach by subsidizing mediocrity and rewarding long service when it is unremarkable. Leadership represents the present and the future, and must always be looking for innovative ways to better serve the people and their interests. Leadership is about winning the medal for the team, not about losing while playing hard. We've got to bring back and support real people who want to be politicians and who are connected with their community. While I believe that we should control our own destiny, our own thought processes, and our own companies, government should do its best to serve the public good and become part of the solution not the problem. I believe that the *Pink Heals Program* can help. But it might ruffle a few feathers. Politicians tell voters what they want to hear. I'm telling politicians what they need to hear.

As it is

Americans are living longer than ever before, and 12.4 percent of the population is over the age of 65. Naturally, healthcare and how to pay for it, will increasingly become an issue as we age. Fifty-one percent of Americans are without health insurance, and with rising unemployment and an unstable economy, that figure is sure to increase. Inevitably, people will get sick, and without insurance, many will face catastrophic financial loss from which most will never recover. Even for those with private or employer provided insurance, the situation is bleak. Medical and prescription drug costs are skyrocketing, while insurance companies are raising premiums to maintain profits, driving the bottom line up for everyone. This results in less disposable income for families and fewer visits to the doctor for preventative diagnostic care, which parlays into a reduction of early detection of cancer and other diseases. This year alone, published estimates warn that nearly 1.6 million women of all ages will be diagnosed with cancer, excluding certain skin cancers, and that 1,500 of them will die each day.

The cost in human life is substantial, but the ancillary effects of cancer are staggering. Every day on tour I meet people who have lost their homes and had their families ripped apart and destroyed by the physical and emotional effects of cancer. I have listened to their stories, felt their anguish, and I have cried with them. But what can we do?

Prevention

"An ounce of prevention is worth a pound of cure," is among the wisest things ever said. Many of our health and societal problems can be avoided or alleviated by following Benjamin Franklin's sage advice, but advice is the easiest thing given and the hardest thing to follow. While we can take personal responsibility for our behavior and make good choices that directly affect our short and long-term physical and mental health, it is difficult to individually control genetics, the environment, the economy, and time. Add to that the human element. We don't always do what is best for us. We overeat. We eat the wrong things. We don't exercise enough. We have bad habits. We make poor choices. The list goes on. Inevitably, we all die despite the lifestyle we led or the choices we made, but while we are still in the game, we must fight on and personally continue to look for ways to improve the quality of life for ourselves and for everyone in our community. Collectively, we can help delay the inevitable and reduce the financial and societal burden of caring for us once we become sick and unable to provide or care for ourselves.

There are no easy answers. We cannot afford to stopping looking for ways to fix or alleviate our problems just because the problems are prevalent and complex. Finding viable ways to meet our needs is not an easy fix, and relying on an aging and crumbling system to fix itself is unrealistic and irresponsible. The time to act is now.

Immediate Care

In addition to the *Pink Heals Program* that is being adopted by communities across the country, I want to go one step further and set up programs at the city level that provide immediate care for people who have been diagnosed with cancer and who have no insurance. Some of the specific points include:

- **100 percent of the funds raised by a tax-based community and all entities are deposited into an account administered by a two-person committee that is paid by the city. The account will be overseen by designated people in the community and open for public review.**
- **100 percent of the funds stay in the program.**
- **100 percent of the funds remain in the community.**
- **100 percent of medical costs will be paid by the fund after insurance.**

Will it work? Who knows, but if cities and communities have to pay for the treatment of cancer after insurance, they will soon be crying the loudest for a cure. It won't be individuals. It will be large, tax-based communities. When they can't make money from us getting sick there's going to be a cry like never before. I'm trying to create an entire mechanism that places the burden of a woman's illness on her community whether they have cancer or not. If they have insurance, there will be a supplemental cancer policy, because even if a person has insurance and gets a rare cancer, they could be financially wiped out in no time. According to the latest Bureau of Labor Statistics, government at all levels, excluding education and hospitals, comprises approximately 8 percent of the work force, with the average state or local government worker receiving $39.83 per hour in wages and benefits compared to $27.49 an hour in the private sector. Clearly, government perpetuates itself and should assume a relatively greater share of the burden. Of course, some might see this as a radical approach, but the conventional approach is flawed and inefficient. And so is the approach to fundraising. There are now a few states in the country where it's written into law that 100 percent of the charitable funds raised in that state have to stay in that state. Large fundraisers are taking millions of dollars out of state to their corporate headquarters, where up to 60-70 percent of the money goes toward the paying of salaries and marketing expenses. Sadly, the citizens of that state are not seeing the direct effect of their money. If each state's attorney general's office, which is the easiest to contact, pushed for a law mandating that all fundraising dollars have to stay within their local communities. If every institution fundraised for its own people and not for corporate charity, they would raise millions for people who are battling cancer. But they have to be forced under the threat of vote. If I drove my pink truck up to Capitol Hill, it would take me twenty years to get anything done, but if I drive around in a pink fire truck and use synergy based on trust and love to selflessly help people, people will notice. And if the politicians don't agree to it, the people will remove them with their votes. I'm building an empire of hope and love not for a cure for cancer, but for immediate care.

Heather

Civic Fundraising

Although cities are not typically in the business of fundraising, they need to be. As we serve our communities, we should implement programs we can own. We should not work for a specific charity. We should own our own labor of love as a city and as a city government, then we can dictate or allow each department to allocate the funds within the community as they deem appropriate. However, it is important that communities understand that promotion is the key to success. Often, billing and promoting a fundraiser as an event to "fight cancer" or to "increase cancer awareness," has a negative effect. Attending an event with a few ladies handing out brochures and promoting awareness is boring. There has to be a hook to get people to attend and it must be packaged properly. If a free wellness fair is organized to celebrate the women in our communities because we recognize that they are the glue of our society, and we collectively raise money for women's issues, particularly cancer, then everyone comes out. There are bouncy rides for kids, skin doctors who check for the skin sun damage,

Pink Heals in front of a B-1 bomber in Abilene, TX.

and perhaps even a free mobile mammography unit, and the event becomes a community wide support effort for women. It brings out politicians, community leaders, and CEOs because they know their women are watching, and that they will support us as we support them, not because they're sick with cancer. Yes, we're raising money. And yes, we're waging battle against this terrorist called cancer on her behalf. But we're also celebrating her as a female and what she means to us in our community. If you don't come out to this event and you don't support it, it could be political suicide.

As a country, we often say, "Why doesn't anyone vote?" and "Why doesn't anyone trust our politicians?" If we implement more programs like this, and the politicians come out and genuinely help the community and apolitically show their support, people will begin trusting them. True, women are a major voting block in the community, and some people will narrowly view politicians who attend the events as currying favor and serving their own interests, but if they selflessly help raise money that stays in their own community, they will be viewed as concerned, caring, and effective leaders.

Pressure from the Bottom

It is the civic responsibility of each citizen to expose inefficiency, waste, corruption, and abuse in all levels of government. This also applies to the insurance and healthcare industries, and to any system, organization, or industry that serves or conducts business with the public and threatens its citizens. We must protect the young, the elderly, the sick, the indigent, and all those who cannot protect themselves. We must advocate for ourselves and others when we can, and empower capable people to advocate for us when we cannot. Individually, this is often difficult, but the collective economic and political strength of a community can have a substantial impact at the marketplace and in the voting booth. But our responsibility does not stop there. We must also be part of the solution.

A central tenet of the *Pink Heals Program* is to increase awareness and to empower people to stand up for themselves, especially when battling cancer and the challenges it presents, while at the same time, drawing from the love, energy, talents, experience, and support of the community.

The first step to individual empowerment is knowledge. We must educate ourselves and learn how to access local and state government agencies and utilize the services they provide. As taxpayers and citizens, we pay for the services and are entitled to them, but local governments don't spend a lot of time and money advertising their services. They leave it up to the citizen to learn how to navigate the system, and often those who are persistent, get the prize.

Besides survival and family issues, one of the most frustrating things that people with cancer endure is dealing with insurance companies. Be proactive. Learn what your rights are and how to file a complaint with the State Department of Insurance (DOI) when you believe an insurance company might be fraudulent, or not complying with the terms of your agreement. Most DOIs can be accessed on the internet and the sites are usually user friendly. An inquiry from the DOI can bring a lot of heat on an insurance company and often produce quick results.

The Office of the State Attorney General is another great resource. Some of its responsibilities are to uniformly and adequately enforce the laws of its state and to protect citizens from fraudulent, unfair, and illegal activities, to include the government itself. It also thrives on going to bat for the underdog since there is no direct financial incentive. What could be better?

Conscientious Capitalism

The quality of healthcare and pharmaceutical drugs available in America is a result of our free market society and is unmatched in the world. But they aren't cheap. The cost of drugs, especially those used in treating cancer, are beyond what most people can pay without insurance, and even then, many insurance companies will not pay for experimental drugs and/ or procedures, or for those drugs and procedures not widely accepted by the medical community or approved by the FDA. Throughout the book, I've stressed the power of community and of individual and collective responsibility, which should not be confused with socialism, communism, entitlement or anything close. I lean neither too far to the left nor too far to the right, and I am a strong believer in capitalism, and in a free and open market economy based on personal initiative, hard work, and competition. Free enterprise has been the backbone of this country and the key to its success for over two hundred years, and as long as we foster and cultivate the entrepreneurial spirit, the best and brightest will continue to come and to provide us with arguably the best of everything.

How much profit is too much? When does the solution to a problem become a larger part of the problem? How do we fix it? Or can we? The Pink Heals Program cannot solve the world's ills. It cannot dictate morality, set profit limits on drugs and services, or place a monetary value on a single life. It cannot topple governments overnight, reduce the price of gas, or cure cancer. Rather, it is a belief system built on traditional values centered upon the notion that women are the core of our society, and that we begin to change by protecting them and celebrating them, and in turn, they heal us.

Women are the strongest economic force in America, and they hold enormous power. They also hold the power to put a conscience in capitalism. With few exceptions, mothers teach their young children the difference between right and wrong and instill in them a strong conscience and moral compass that serves them well for the rest of their lives. Women can instill (or enforce) that same sense of "conscience" in the medical marketplace by marshaling together and using their pocketbooks. No lesson is better learned than an expensive one.

Let's make this our goal.

CHAPTER 9
A PINK FUTURE

Most of the book has looked at the past with an eye toward the future. My nature resists looking back, but sometimes it is important to see where you've been to know where you're going. And after several months of forced reflection, it is clear that the *Pink Heals Program* is headed in the right direction. Barely four years in existence, it has grown tremendously and has offered hope and provided real assistance to tens of thousands of people across the country. We have only begun to scratch the surface of our potential, but we also realize that time and energy are finite, and that the *Pink Heals Program* can only do so much so fast. In addition to conducting our ongoing mission of offering hope to women battling cancer and increasing awareness, the *Pink Heals Program* must always look forward to the future in hopes of finding new and innovative ways to inspire more people to commit their time and effort toward supporting the women we love. Hop on and we hope you enjoy the ride.

Pink Fire Station

As a firefighter for 22 years, I learned that every fire truck has to have a fire station to park in, and that the logical growth of the *Pink Heals Program* is to build a Pink Fire Station based on the same value system as the program itself. Everybody knows what is happening when they see a fire truck rolling down the road. Someone needs rescued, and once the mission is complete, the truck always returns home to its firehouse of brick and steel. But what if the firehouse were built out of souls? What if every brick, beam, piece of flooring, and everything in it bore the name of someone who had battled cancer? It would become a memorial unlike any other.

Aerial view of Pink Heals Fire Station.

In 2009, I had the RRM Design Group in San Luis, Obispo, California draw up concept plans for a Pink Heals Station. The design team of Kirk Van Cleave, David Chacon, and Kirstie Acevedo did a wonderful job and captured the spirit of what I envisioned. Strategically, the idea is to build a Pink Fire Station in 10-12 counties around the country that have taken the *Pink Heals Program* and used it for the betterment of their communities and to give it to them. The station would not be the color pink, but would be symbolic in honor of the women of that community and their families who are constantly battling cancer, and although it would house pink fire trucks, it would not be an operational firehouse. Each station would be staffed and operated by volunteers from the fire and police departments who would take the trucks out into the community and attend fundraisers, and when they would receive a call that a woman was diagnosed with cancer, they would deliver flowers and a hug to her. The station would also be used as a conference center to organize fundraising and charitable events and operate as a full-service wellness center for women where people could meet with health professionals, exercise, give and attend classes, cook, or have support group meetings.

Front view of Pink Heals Fire Station.

Funds for construction will be raised in several ways. Over time, as the Pink Heals Program builds synergy and trust with people throughout the country, it will sell memorial bricks. Donors will purchase various sizes of bricks and provide the name they wish to have imprinted on them, along with a brief message.

Pink Heals Fire Station Plaza.

Education

Education is another area where the Pink Heals concept will make an impact. In fact, one progressive school district in California accepted the program during the 2011 Mother's Day Tour and plans to implement it beginning in the fall. If I were a teacher, I would spend a portion of my summer helping people celebrate making a difference and inspiring the country to get on board a program to help our kids. As adults, all of us need to instill a sense of service in our children and to stop adopting the "me first" attitude. We need to teach them through leadership, mentorship, and service to others that we uplift ourselves, and by empowering others, we make ourselves stronger, contrary to the tired perception that compassion makes us weak and servile. The teachers, coaches, and mentors in my life from grade school through now have made a profound impact in my life, and I would not have accomplished what I have without them. Every child needs and deserves the same attention, effort, guidance, and experience that positive adult role models can give. If our society is truly to change for the better, the time for action is now.

Our new logo for educators.

Our message to parents, teachers, and school administrators is to empower the individual schools and their students to start wearing the pink shirts and to start celebrating their community by selling the shirts and giving the money to a local organization that helps the women in their own community. It won't be the state superintendent of schools ordering all schools to give to the American Cancer Society or to *Susan G. Komen*; each principal will allow their own students to create their own tee shirt logos; to produce and sell their own shirts; and to decide collectively who in the community receives the money. By empowering each school, politics are largely eliminated and individual initiative rewarded. More importantly, the school leadership is trusting and empowering its students to be good leaders, creative entrepreneurs, and to be selfless.

Since this program is in its infancy, we'd love to hear ideas from students, teachers, administrators, and parents how the *Pink Heals Program* might help your local schools. Our children are the future and our greatest natural resource, and the time to invest in them is now.

Pink China

The People's Republic of China has 1.34 billion people, and some 533 million are women who are dying to go pink. With the world's largest female population, establishing a Pink Heals presence in China is one of my greatest goals. And given the lower status of its women and the reluctance of the male dominated leadership to surrender its voice, it will perhaps be my greatest challenge as well.

But can or will an ancient and proud nation sustain a program that puts women first? Not all countries can. Some are very patriarchal and the notion that women come first is still 200 years away, but China has shown the ability to adapt and change when it needed to. The symbolism of being allowed to open a chapter in the world's largest communist state would be immense, not just for us, but for the Chinese leadership as well. With an acute shortage of women, China is already feeling the jagged effects of a male dominated society, and any efforts to empower and improve the status and condition of women, no matter how subtle, would be viewed by many as step forward.

Initially, I want to meet with Chinese officials and to assure them that we're not trying to overthrow their government, abolish communism, or change their way of life by impressing our own value system. My first objective is to meet with like-minded individuals, locate a fire truck, paint it pink, have some tee shirts made, and take a photo on the Great Wall. Baby steps.

See you soon!

EPILOGUE

I am 48 years old and I might die tomorrow. Or I might live another 40 years. Who knows? But however long I have left on planet earth, I don't want to leave a house to my kids. I want to leave a legacy to my children. It's not about what's in my bank account. It's not about the truck I drive, the friends I have, or the job I hold. Every day for 22 years I marched off to my blue collar job; firefighter. Employee number 06310. City of Glendale. But there's more to life than living to work. Even if you're a teacher, a lawyer, a policeman, or even a professional athlete, we weren't put here just to be somebody's employee. We were put here to make a difference. Can you imagine if everyone thought that way? Can you imagine if we all marched like this? My kids love me and I'm gone three months a year on tour. I can use them as an excuse not to go, but it wouldn't wash. I could have a hundred kids and they'd all feel loved. But there are people dying out there. People suffering. There are people who don't have kids. There are people who have kids and can't take care of them. There are people who are homeless. There are people who are sick with cancer. We can do about anything we want if we decide to. Four years ago, I decided to make a difference for as I long as I could.

At the end of each day if the moon isn't pink I've failed. And that's what motivates me, knowing that I have to get out there tomorrow and to make a difference. If I touch two people one day, I've got to reach three the next, and four the next. That's the way I am, and I've learned to accept it. I hope that most people who've read this book overlooked my honesty, optimism, and naïveté, and appreciated the spirit of my story and what I'm trying to accomplish with the *Pink Heals Program*. After reading this book, some people will be inspired to adopt the program in their own community, and others will not. But whichever camp you fall into, I encourage you to take action and to reach beyond what others say is your grasp. Join the program or start one of your own. Dare to be different. Challenge authority when it abuses or is ineffective. Don't take "no" for an answer before the question is asked. The nine innings of our lives go by quickly, and we must be prepared to go into the game when the game calls. But more importantly, we must compete if we are to win. Now grab a bat and let's play ball! I'll pitch.

May 31, 2011 – The cake says it all!

The end…and the beginning.

Appendix

Pink Heals Drivers

Josh Baker	FL	Greg McAlister	TX
James Barbeau	IL	Jeff McCarroll	AZ
Robert Bidwell	CT	Ryan McMurray	OH
Denver Bierstedt	TX	Jaime McPhilomy	FL
Jason Birrenkott	ND	Brad Magness	TX
Steve Bogle	AZ	Joel Mains	IL
Steve Cannon	AZ	Andy Mhley	PA
Dave Cherrone	IN	Wally Monsivaiz	NM
Chris Chomel	TX	Mike Mullins	VA
Gary Cochran	TX	Philip Newbauer	SC
Mark Colin	AZ	Scott Phillips	AZ
Tim Cordin	AZ	Mike Prosi	IL
Ted Dion	RI	Steve Rusin	IL
Dave Gardner	MO	Carlos Schulz	AZ
Judy Geier	CT	Shane Shifflett	GA
Wendell Geigle	TX	Jonathan Smith	NC
Antonio Gonzales	TX	Tommy Taylor	AZ
Jared Hobson	AZ	James Thompson	OH
Jay Holt	TX	Christopher Torres	NM
Richard Janne	KS	Jay Young	TX
Meredith Lund	NH		

Photos

*Special thanks to all those who provided photos and artwork for the book.

The Authors

Dave Graybill (pictured with son David and daughter Lauren) still lives in the Phoenix area but can be found driving a pink fire truck on a highway somewhere in the USA.

Lance Zedric is a noted author, historian, and teacher, and is a former U.S. Army intelligence analyst. He lives with his family in Illinois. For more information about Lance, visit his website at www.LanceZedric.com

Pink Heals

Check Out

Pink Heals Apparel

At

PINKFIRETRUCKS.ORG

Pink Heals